The Small Business Advantage

JUSTIN G KINNEAR

Copyright © 2013 Justin G Kinnear

All rights reserved.

ISBN: 1493698435
ISBN-13: 978-1493698431

DEDICATION

To Paula, Andrew and Robert
for your unending support and confidence.

CONTENTS

	ACKNOWLEDGEMENTS	i
	PREFACE	iii
	INTRODUCTION	vi
1	WHEN IT COMES TO CUSTOMER SERVICE, WHAT SHOULD SMALL BUSINESSES BE DOING?	1
2	THE FOUNDATION OF FAILURE: CREATING A TERRIBLE FIRST IMPRESSION	3
3	THE NEXT LAYER OF FAILURE: LETTING YOUR STANDARDS DROP	13
4	CEMENTING FAILURE: CHANGING FOCUS WHEN YOU GROW	28
5	HOME TRUTHS ABOUT YOUR CUSTOMERS	42
6	LAYING THE FOUNDATIONS FOR RECOVERY	50
7	THE RIGHT EMPLOYEES AND THE RIGHT MANAGEMENT	61
8	IDENTIFY WHAT IS CRITICALLY IMPORTANT	65
9	KEEP YOUR BEST PEOPLE CLOSE TO THE CUSTOMER	77
10	MAPPING THE CUSTOMER SERVICE SYSTEM	89
11	UNDERSTANDING YOUR REALITY	99
12	COME UP WITH A PLAN AND SHARE IT	109
13	MEASURE, CORRECT AND KEEP TRYING	115
	CONCLUSION	120

ACKNOWLEDGMENTS

I would like to acknowledge all the people who have contributed, each in their own way, to the completion of this book. I especially thank Andrea Mitchell, my editor, for her painstaking attention to detail and rigorous challenge without which there would be far less clarity.

In no particular order I also want to pay tribute to Alan McDonald, Alison Hand, Grainne Higgins, Liam Carey, Bryan Gobbett, Joe Sweeney, Liam McKenna Sr., David Cornick, Pat Cannon, Paul Kinsella, Jill Whitlock, Frank Condon, Dermot Duff and Paul Burnell for their own unique contributions to this piece of work.

The cover image is provided very generously by Kelly Sikkema. Sincere thanks for permitting me to use your image Kelly.

PREFACE

Great customer service has become mythical and elusive - like the Loch Ness monster it is almost the stuff of legend. And just like the Loch Ness monster many people try hard to find great customer service, some even traveling great distances in the hope of enjoying even a glimpse of it. Most return home disappointed.

Nowadays it is more likely that you will encounter examples of great customer service in a book or on a blog, or perhaps you might hear an experience described at a conference or in a conversation between friends or colleagues. How can it be that great customer service has become so rare and elusive? Great customer service is what keeps customers coming back time and again. Without great customer service, a business will slowly and steadily lose its customers, leading to the certain death of the business.

Who can save great service from certain death?

Business owners, managers and employees all have an opportunity to save customer service from certain death. As a business owner you can be the foundation of great service. Your intuition tells you how important it is to hold on to the customers you already have. If customers expect a mediocre service experience you know they won't stay loyal to you and your business. Instead, imagine a future where your business stands head and shoulders above your competitors by consistently delivering great customer service, the kind of service that your customers talk enthusiastically about when they meet friends, family and colleagues. This should be the future you strive for.

Perhaps you are a manager or supervisor working in a business that provides goods or services to customers. You also know how important it is to keep your customers satisfied so that they come back time and again.

You too can save great customer service from death. If you are going to save great customer service then you need to get serious about it. Imagine a future where the people you lead are at the top of their profession when it comes to delivering a consistent high standard of customer service. In that future customers choose to do business with your business because you are providing a valued experience every time, an experience that cannot be matched by your competitors. Imagine a time where customers are willing to overlook an occasional misstep by you or even pay higher prices just because they enjoy doing business with you. How great would that be?

Perhaps you are an employee working in a customer-facing role. Imagine a future where you enjoy a relationship of mutual respect with virtually all your customers, where dealing with customers is consistently enjoyable. Imagine a future where your customers frequently tell you how much they value what you do for them. Can you imagine coming in to work every day in that reality?

If you are a business owner, a manager, or someone responsible for providing customer service to customers then this book is written specially for you. Delivering great customer service means you need to get serious about service. But this book won't teach you how to pay lip service. The ideas I'm about to set out here will require more than developing a formulaic approach to handling customers. Great service is not about providing sensitivity training or teaching staff to smile and it's definitely not about standing up when speaking on the telephone. It's certainly not about large-scale expensive consultancy-based projects that involve retraining everyone in your business.

In the pages ahead you'll learn what it takes to establish authentic customer service, the kind of great service that shows your customers you actually *do* want their business and *do* want to keep them. And most importantly, you will learn how to develop authentic customer service that is consistent and that lasts.

The history of business is dotted with examples of businesses that delivered great customer service for a time but then lapsed back to providing mediocre or awful service. If you throw enough money and energy at a business it's easy to change things for a little while. It's much harder to change something for good. This book is about changing customer service for good. Great customer service requires consistency and authenticity and this will take some time to get right. If you manage to get it right it can make all the difference to you and your customers and secure your right to your customers' loyalty.

If you are serious about keeping your customers and thriving in the future then you need to think and act seriously when it comes to serving your customers. Over the coming pages I will bring you to a point of sharp focus and clarity about what needs to happen if you want to fix the way you provide customer service today. I aim to show you how it's possible for great customer service to be re-born and how you can make customer service the key difference maker that keeps your customers coming back for more when everyone else's customers are defecting.

Justin G. Kinnear
Dublin, Ireland.

INTRODUCTION

On October 14th 2011 the website Business Insider[1] carried the headline "The 18 most hated companies in America: They've given up on customer service". It is tragic to see well-known companies such as Bank of America and Delta Air Lines appearing on a list like this, having fallen dramatically from grace and not looking likely to ever get their reputations back. But the companies on this list were all big companies. What about small companies? Have small companies given up on customer service too?

In my estimation, customer service is in a terrible state in both big and small companies. Not only that, it's terrible in almost every part of the world. Not enough companies care about customer service anymore, and it shows in the way their customers speak about them. At the same time, most companies still say that customer service is important, and still believe that it can make all the difference when trying to win or keep a customer from a competitor.

It is one thing to say that you value customer service. It's another thing altogether to actually do it. An old maxim teaches us that strategy isn't what you say you'll do, it's what you actually do. In the same way, your commitment to customer service will be judged by how you actually deliver customer service.

Over the course of my career I have worked in big international businesses, and I have worked in small, local businesses. For many years I was a consultant to CEOs, entrepreneurs, managers, scientists and many others. I have witnessed the spending of millions and millions of dollars and over a hundred thousand hours of training directed at the problem of customer service. I have seen billion-dollar CRM and state-of-the-art telephone systems installed in the hope of improving the customer experience. I have seen it all fail to do the one thing they all set out to do: improve customer service.

I watched as great minds and great leaders made decision after decision that made no sense. A training programme that taught staff to stand up when speaking on the phone, another programme that taught staff how to smile, and yet another that taught staff techniques about how to make conversations with customers last longer. All resulted in customers noticing that staff were behaving inauthentically, and all resulted in customers thinking that service had become worse and not better. Looking at these efforts at the time, I hoped that somehow things would improve because of all the investment and energy being spent. But things did not improve.

That's when I decided to do something about the waste of money and energy, the misguided efforts and the misunderstandings about customers and what customers want. I decided to write this book. I knew that I had to suggest something different about how customer service could be improved. I knew that at its core, providing great customer service is simple and intuitive. I set out to capture my thoughts on how to create great customer service and how to keep it going over time.

This book has a number of simple purposes. First, it will help you really understand what we mean when we describe bad customer service. You will come to know how terrible things really are for customers today.

Next the book will challenge you to define why customer service matters to you and your business. If you don't really care about customer service, it's better to find that out now before you waste time and effort on something that you will ultimately walk away from.

Then the book will show you how to assess the kind of customer service you are providing today, and where you have weaknesses that are damaging the customer's experience and your reputation.

You will learn how to build the right kind of customer service system, how to keep it intact and sustain it over time so that your organisation can deliver a consistently good experience.

Finally, you'll learn how to stop yourself from interfering with customer service in the name of progress.

The book is primarily written for owners of small businesses and managers who work in small businesses. If you are an employee who works in a small business there are some nuggets in here for you too. If you are an owner or manager in a larger business there are plenty of transferable insights as well. Basically, if you have a genuine interest in better customer service you'll find the ideas contained in these pages to be of value.

In addition to my own experience, I have drawn insights from the worlds of customer service training, general business, management and leadership, quality management, process improvement, production management, innovation and creativity, psychology, sociology, neuroscience, neuromarketing, human resources, consulting, sales and marketing. The ideas contained in this book blend together only those aspects that add something useful to the improvement of customer service. In doing so I rebut some long standing practices and cherished ideas in some of these fields. I make no apologies for that.

I am optimistic about this book's capacity to help anyone in business to drive real change in the way we handle our customers. Customers deserve better and I am confident that if you adopt some of my ideas that your customers will notice.

I suggest that you go slowly and read a little at a time. It would be useful to keep a notepad and a pen beside you and to make notes about any ideas that you would like to take away and explore.

After each section you should stop and ask yourself some hard questions. I'd suggest asking "do we treat customers this way?" or "how could I find out if we are guilty of this annoying practice?"

I have placed summary points at the end of each section with some provocative questions for you to ponder. I recommend that you copy or tear out these pages and keep them close to hand for quick reference.

If you have a team of people working for you, no matter how small, it would be a good idea to explore these issues and ideas together. Be brave and be willing to listen to your team's insights. You may be amazed.

While preparing this book I was often overcome with doubt and worried that someone else had written a similar book with ideas just like mine. While there are hundreds of books on the market on the subject of customer service, sadly, most cover the same ground and suggest the same approaches as all those training courses I spoke about earlier in this introduction. I have yet to find another book on the subject of customer service that suggests what I suggest in these pages. You will find in these pages that my approach is not based on shaping (or forcing) your employees to behave in a certain way. My approach is based on a very simple foundation. Start with the right people. With the right people on board, you can build up your business from there and create something amazing. With the wrong people on board, you have no chance of creating great customer service. I'll build from there to show you those things you can and must do in order to make service better.

1 WHEN IT COMES TO CUSTOMER SERVICE, WHAT SHOULD SMALL BUSINESSES BE DOING?

When describing great customer service most books tend to cite examples from the world of big business. With so much focus on the big examples you might be forgiven for thinking that only big business can deliver a truly outstanding customer service experience.

In truth a great customer service experience is not the preserve of big business. Small businesses have a scale that makes them more nimble. Small businesses typically have far fewer layers, meaning they tend to be closer to the customer. And they are sufficiently small that changing something important is nowhere near as complex and onerous as it might be inside a big business. With the widespread availability of new forms of communication and information delivery, small businesses are now better placed to deliver outstanding customer service experiences. This should be the case, but the typical customer service experience is almost universally poor.

It is easy to offer examples of great customer service from global hotel chains or upscale department stores. The difficulty comes when we try to be precise about what exactly defines a great customer service experience. What makes for a great experience in a luxury hotel may not have the same effect in a local sports store. When you try to piece together a pattern to describe what makes for great customer service experiences across different types and sizes of businesses you can quickly run into difficulty.

Most small businesses know customer service can be the difference maker that determines if the customer will come back or not. However, inside small businesses customer service is often poorly planned and poorly executed.

While big business can afford to spend vast sums on CRM systems, customer loyalty programmes, and global employee training programmes, small businesses simply can't do that. The good news is that you don't need to spend vast sums of money to create an outstanding customer service experience in a small business. Instead what is required is much simpler and far less costly. There are steps to follow to get your customer service in shape and to start creating the kind of experiences that quickly get noticed by your customers.

This book is based on the idea that small business customer service should be affordable and reasonably easy to implement and sustain. It should be practical and easy to manage. It should be scalable, growing with you as your business improves and grows. It should be repeatable and consistent from employee to employee, store to store and day to day. And above all it should be valuable. It should be a unique part of why your customers choose to come back time and time again.

Customer service is not about CRM, loyalty programmes or employee training. It's not about fabled stories or customer service legends. And it's certainly not about introducing systems, processes, procedures and red tape. Customer service in the world of small business is about making customers feel good about doing business with you. This book will show you how to think and act smart in your business so you can get all the benefits of great customer service without committing precious spending resources on expensive systems or programmes.

However before we start exploring how to make customer service great inside your business it is important to spend a little time understanding what exactly the problem is with customer service today. This book starts by identifying the things that businesses do which cause real and lasting damage to the customer service experience and to the reputation of a business.

One final point. While the focus of the book is on small businesses the ideas presented here have just as much significance and applicability in the world of big business. Great customer service should be simple because great business is simple. Let me lead you there.

PAUSE AND THINK

To get the most from this book I recommend that you pause every time you see one of these 'PAUSE AND THINK' headings. At each one you will find a question, suggestion or action that you should consider for your own business.

2 THE FOUNDATION OF FAILURE: CREATING A TERRIBLE FIRST IMPRESSION

For most things in life there is a very fine line that separates the great from the ordinary. Often it's only an extra ounce of effort that makes all the difference between an outstanding achievement and a mediocre performance. Customer service is no different. It will only take a tiny extra effort to create an experience that a customer will be delighted to talk about with everyone they know.

The flip side is that you don't have to work too hard to mess it all up. Businesses often spend time and money investing in customer service training and systems and infrastructure but then undo it all by not paying attention to a few small details. Sadly these are the few small details that make all the difference to the customer. This simple failing is extremely common and has become a global phenomenon at this stage.

The good news, though, is that businesses tend to mess things up in a fairly predictable and narrow set of ways in just about every country in the world, which gives some cause for optimism. By identifying the ways that businesses repeatedly spoil the customer service experience we can focus on eliminating these practices and reversing the damage. Getting rid of those damaging practices sets the scene for great customer service to become the key factor that differentiates you from your competitors.

Finding the hole in your boat

As a small business owner responsible for keeping the customers you have and attracting new customers, you need to pay careful attention to the problems you have today. Bad customer service is like having a hole in your boat. No amount of repainting or adding new and clever features is going to keep you above water for long. Ultimately if you want your business performance to improve you've got to start by repairing the hole in your boat. This means that you've got to work hard to find out what aspects of the way you provide service to your customers are sinking your business and destroying relationships.

We'll begin by looking at three annoying habits of businesses today that damage the customer experience: Pointing out that your customer is wrong; acting like you don't care when really you do; and making customers wish they were somewhere else. These three tend to happen very early in the customer's relationship with your business and create a very poor first impression. As you read about them, ask yourself if you recognize these behaviours in your business, or as a customer of someone else's business.

Annoying Habit No. 1

Pointing out that your customer is wrong

In business we like to think that we always have the customer's best interests at heart. It hurts, therefore, when a customer comes into your business and claims that they have been wronged or that somehow your business failed to honor a commitment. Naturally it is important to find out if this is true or not. Nobody enjoys being accused of shoddy work or being unprofessional. This is especially true when you know you're right about a situation involving an unhappy customer.

When a customer walks into your business and complains about something, one approach might be to immediately comply and let the customer have what they want. It's often the easiest way to remedy a customer problem. Realistically, no business can afford to give in every time a customer complains or is demanding. This kind of policy would effectively reward customers for complaining, setting a dangerous and costly precedent and would quickly force you out of business.

However, sometimes there is a place for taking the long view, the view that says it might just be worth yielding in the interests of keeping a customer or of avoiding an unsavory incident on your premises.

> John, a university student, works part-time in a big electrical store selling various small appliances. It's Christmas and very busy in the store. John advises a customer about a small portable sound system for his daughter. Like most dads when buying for daughters, the customer is anxious. John carefully explains the various models and suggests the best fit. Satisfied, the customer pays for the unit and leaves the shop.
>
> The day after Christmas John notices the same customer entering the store, his face bright red and angry. John approaches him and asks, "Have you run into some trouble?" "I have" he says and proceeds to explain that when his daughter opened her Christmas present and inserted the batteries it did not work. Examining the radio, John opens the battery door and finds the problem. The batteries are all inserted the wrong way round. John takes out the batteries, places them on the counter, and then replaces them one by one. He pushes the power button. Music!
>
> The customer's face had turned red again but this time from embarrassment. The customer said, "I don't understand". John suggested that perhaps the batteries had simply not made proper contact and that it was likely that was all that was wrong. John showed him the contacts in the battery compartment and suggests that when loading new batteries it is important to push them in firmly. The customer thanked John as he helped him pack up the unit into the original box and quickly exited the store.

In situations like this it's easy to apportion blame to the customer. It would have been easy to say, "You fool! You've put the batteries in the wrong way round" but what purpose would that serve? The customer would likely become embarrassed and angry. The perception of poorly written instructions, coupled with annoyance at having driven all the way to the store, will now be making him feel foolish. Is that really the lasting impression of your business that you want to create in your customer's mind?

The need to show the customer that they are wrong can become really extreme. When behaviour goes that far it can take you into dangerous territory, the territory where customers start reaching for their legal advisor's phone number. Consider this example.

> A customer took a leather mobile phone case back to the store where it was bought as a gift. When unpacked it was clear the item was not new and was badly scuffed and worn. Upon presentation of the proof of purchase the store assistant offered to replace the product without hesitation, however, as the item was out of stock the store assistant asked the customer to call back in a couple of days when stock was replenished.
>
> Attempts at securing a replacement continued unsuccessfully for a number of weeks. Numerous drop-in visits to the store were made and phone calls placed to check if a replacement was now available. Finally the store called the customer to say that the item was now back in stock and that he should come in and pick up a replacement product.
>
> Upon arriving at the store the customer was informed that there was in fact no replacement product available. Having now waited patiently for several weeks and having made numerous attempts to secure a replacement, the customer was losing patience and decided to ask for a refund. The store assistant advised the customer that this was not possible so the customer asked to speak to a manager. The manager appeared and asked if she could help. Rather than attempting to address the way the store had been inconveniencing the customer, the manager suggested instead that the customer was perhaps not entirely honest about why the case was damaged, suggesting that the customer might be trying to secure an unwarranted replacement of a case that he himself had damaged The customer now become irate and insisted on a refund if the store was unable to provide him with a replacement. The manager refused suggesting that there was not enough cash in the register to refund the cost of the product. In a desperate act the customer stated that he would not leave the store until he received a refund at which point the store manager threatened to call security to have him thrown out of the store!

It is bad enough that a customer has been inconvenienced and has their time wasted making fruitless journeys into a store. To compound that shabby treatment with an argument about who is right and who is wrong is pointless and ultimately damaging to the relationship between the store and customer. This problem might have been resolved if the store assistant and store manager had thought about whether it made sense to give a refund at the beginning, and in doing so potentially keep a customer for future business. Treating an existing customer in this shabby manner makes the chances of this customer (or anyone they have shared this story with) unlikely to do business with that store for quite some time, if ever again.

Sometimes it is smarter to apologize even though you believe yourself to be 100% right about your facts. If you want your customer to remain your customer, then you really must let them know that you value them more than you value the item or service they bought from you. Sadly what is often valued most is the particular transaction. Valuing the customer means that you value the person and not just what they have in their wallet. It is that obvious. If you're doing this right your customer should have a better impression of your business every time they conclude business with you.

Hold on to the customers you already have

Most sales people know that it costs more to sell something to a new customer than it does to sell the same thing to an existing customer. With new customers you have to spend time, money and effort getting their attention, marketing to them, and building up their interest. Existing customers know who you are and what you do. And if you're doing it right they already respect and trust you. So why would you choose to get into a disagreement with a valued customer just to prove a point about who is right? The received wisdom in sales is that it costs five times more to sell something to a new customer than it does to an existing customer. Correspondingly the more the item in question costs the more costly it is to attract the customer in the first place. So don't pick a fight with your customers unless it really is a fight worth picking.

To avoid pointing out that your customer is wrong

When a situation like this arises don't see it as a choice of keeping the money or keeping the customer. If necessary, be willing to apologize and do it early in the discussion. The earlier you apologize, the more of the customer's goodwill towards your business you save.

PAUSE AND THINK

What happens in your business when a customer complains? What is the most important outcome today for you and your employees?

Annoying Habit No. 2

Acting like you don't care when really you do

Most countries have laws that protect the rights of customers when they buy goods and services. These laws set out what customers are entitled to should the product or service they purchase fail to do as advertised. Most include a simple explanation of the circumstances in which a customer might be entitled to a refund. It usually works like this: If, in order to sell a product to you, I tell you something about the product's capabilities that are plainly wrong, and you find out soon after that the product you bought does not in fact do what I led you to believe it could, then you are entitled to a refund.

Likewise, if I sell you something and it is damaged, or broken, or defective, or does not work properly, then clearly a refund would be in order. These laws offer good protections to customers under normal conditions, since customers can take comfort in the fact that they have a period of time after the purchase within which their rights as consumers are protected.

Some retailers have adopted a more flexible approach to product returns and exchanges in order to be more customer-friendly. In some cases retailers actively encourage customers to bring items back if they have simply changed their minds. In other cases stores make it possible to bring the item back to the same store chain but in a different city. This is real progress, but not all businesses see this as a positive step. Bizarrely, some retailers continue to adopt an approach to customer service that is closer to what you would expect when buying something out of a suitcase in an alleyway.

More than money

Successful retailers know that there is more to success than making money. They know that the key to good business is not simply to find lots of customers but to find lots of customers who buy today and then come back time and time again to buy something. You can't build a long-term business if you don't plan on having loyal customers because, frankly, you are likely to run out of customers. You'll find the same premise applies in many other sales contexts, whether it's buying a new car, staying in a particular hotel chain or flying with a preferred airline. They all want you to feel so well looked after that you will instantly consider making the same choice next time around. Loyal customers buy more. Existing customers buy more. So to sell more, you've got to treat your customers well and make sure they are satisfied. Consider this example.

Michelle is getting ready to go a sale at a local fashion retail store. The store has two big sales events every year, one just after Christmas and another in the mid-summer. Sometimes excited shoppers camp out the night before the sales events to avail of their famous discounts. Once the doors open on sales event days it's a scramble as shoppers dart left and right, some seeking out particular items and others randomly flicking through clothes rail after clothes rail looking for something that catches their eye. Often clothes end up in heaps on the floor as shoppers rampage through the store seeking the best bargains. The store looks very different during these sales events. During a sale event signs appear that read "No Refund on Items Purchased During the Sale".

Contrast this type of sale event with what's happening across town at another store where loyal customers have been invited to a special preview sale event. At this sale event the doors are closed to regular shoppers and the most loyal customers are invited to come and browse at their leisure, with personal shopping assistants available and courtesy snacks and refreshments provided by the store.

'NO REFUND ON SALE ITEMS' signs often appear around stores during seasonal sales. Customers could interpret a sign like this to mean that normal service does not apply. From a distance, a store may appear to care more about customers during normal business conditions than it does during the seasonal sales period. If you do care about your customers then it makes sense to think about what you are communicating, intentionally or unintentionally, and at all times to your customers. If you want them to be loyal then they should feel that you value them all the time, including during a big sale event.

Most customers don't want to have to work hard to attract a member of staff's attention in a store. They don't want to flag down their server or catch the gaze of a distant and detached employee rooted behind a display counter. They want to be acknowledged and greeted the moment they enter your premises, because they just might be the best thing that happens to you that day. If you don't make your best effort to make customers feel welcome and don't even attempt to do business with them then you have no chance. Customers might just want to browse, and that should be fine. Just don't make assumptions about them, their motives and their real purchasing intent.

The big ocean mental trap

Salespeople can suffer from the view that there are plenty more customers out there. They can suffer from the mistaken belief that the customer needs the seller way more than the seller needs the customer. Marketers might try and convince you of that. At the end of the day, in a market with multiple options and multiple sellers, each seller can't afford to view customers like this. If you're in business to close deals and make profits then you need to think hard about the way you see customers. Clearly, if you work in specialized sales or work with a small fixed group of customers then you do need to fix your gaze on that small group. If, however, you work in the kind of business where everyone that walks in the door could be your customer, then you need to sharpen up. You can't treat customers as if you couldn't care less if they bought something from you.

Finally if we accept that people buy from people that they like, ask yourself how many of your friends would behave like some sellers behave towards their customers? How many of your friends would refuse to acknowledge you when you entered their home, or their office? How many of your friends would allow you to stand unattended for ten minutes? This is not how to do things in the sales world. When customers come in you need to look sharp and get moving.

PAUSE AND THINK

Are there situations during the year where you treat your customer in a different way than you normally would? Big sale times are often when there are temptations to let standards and quality drop in an attempt to maximize short-term business. Think carefully about messages you communicate to customers through signs and displays, and sense-check them with someone you trust to pick out ambiguity or hidden messages.

☐

Annoying Habit No. 3

Making customers wish they were somewhere else

Many people work in jobs where they deal directly with large numbers of customers every day. From time to time an employee may voice the opinion that their job would be easier if customers would disappear. This attitude comes from the belief that customers are unreasonable, want to deliberately make trouble, and don't care about the impact of their behaviour. Thankfully, it's a belief that can be easily challenged and changed for the good of the customer.

> Tom was out driving with his wife on a pleasant Sunday afternoon. They decided to stop for a coffee. When they got inside the place was busy, as the end of the afternoon was approaching. There were two coffee shops inside the building, one at each end of the building. Tom approached the smaller coffee shop where three ladies were filling teapots, pouring coffee and serving cakes to customers. As Tom arrived at the counter there were two or three people in line in front of him. Tom joined the line and waited.
> A lady appeared from behind the counter and hurried over to the end of the line in which Tom was waiting. She quickly moved some chairs into a neat row behind Tom, blocking the path of others wishing to join the queue.
> All this took place without a word being uttered by the lady moving the chairs. Tom interpreted this movement of chairs to be a message for any new arrivals to go to the larger coffee shop at the far end of the building and not to join the line in which Tom stood. The lady then went back behind the counter and resumed her business of serving customers.
> Moments later, a gentleman appeared next to Tom. The gentleman looked into the display cabinet, glanced at the line, and then proceeded to squeeze between the chairs with his wife to join the line. Another couple quickly followed him, also side-stepping the chairs. Tom's eyes diverted towards the lady behind the counter. Her face was a picture of annoyance, aggravation and anger. She was fuming. Tom couldn't hear what she was saying to her colleagues behind the counter but it certainly was not complimentary. Her eyes burned furiously as she gazed at the two couples that had just bypassed her line of chairs. Tom watched her serving the next customer, all the time staring at the end of the line, desperate that nobody else should join the end of the line. Her failed attempt to close the small coffee shop had made Tom wish he had never stopped in.

It definitely is good to go home. Most people can understand an employee's desire to put on their coat and leave at the end of the working day. So what's the problem in this example? Well to begin with how are customers supposed to interpret a line of chairs? From the employee's point of view the chairs are clearly saying "no entry". From a customer's point of view a line of chairs is just a line of chairs. It's ambiguous.

Sometimes it can seem that people who get paid to serve customers really dislike customers. In some cases customers misread the intentions of the person serving them. Customers are not mind readers and won't ever be able to interpret the subtle signs given off by employees in quite the way that employees think they can. This could have been resolved if the employees behind the counter had done a better job of communicating that the small coffee shop closed at 4:30 PM.

Today's way of doing business has evolved over many years to a point of increasing passivity towards customers. Now businesses want it all. They want customers to pour into the store when they are ready to sell, but want customers to stay away early in the morning, towards the end of the evening, and when sales people just aren't in the mood to talk to customers. This can't work. Customers come in to the store when they come in, and good businesses realize that and are ready. Good businesses will take the business whenever the customer wants to do business.

PAUSE AND THINK

Try to imagine yourself in your customer's position. Think about how you could make your intentions clearer to your customer and how you could eliminate any ambiguity in what you are communicating. Take a deep breath and think before you engage your customers. Notice when you are becoming angry and impatient and don't take it out on your customer.

3 THE NEXT LAYER OF FAILURE: LETTING YOUR STANDARDS DROP

As a business owner it is wonderful to watch your business grow and progress over time. As the months pass, more and more people get to hear about you and your business and you might be tempted to give yourself a pat on the back for a job well done. This is a dangerous time for a business because complacency can set in. Employees from the top to the bottom of the company stop paying attention to the little details and standards start to slip. Of course if you are very busy you might not notice this slip in standards. You might believe you and your employees are doing things in exactly the same way that you have always done things.

We all get tired. We all suffer from a drop in energy from time to time. We all need re-energizing and a chance to refocus on what we should be doing. Sadly many businesses don't even realize that their standards have slipped. They don't realize that employees are fatigued. Worse still, they don't know that customers have detected a change in the way the business is operating. Customers will notice very quickly that things are not the same as before. As a small business you need to pay particular attention to any change in the customer experience that you are providing. If you don't it could be doing irreparable damage to your reputation.

Annoying Habit No. 4

Not listening to your customer

In business it makes sense to strive for the perfect customer experience. It also makes the same kind of intuitive sense to strive for efficiency. This drives modern businesses to invest in clever IT systems, call centers of smart people, and tightly-defined processes and procedures to make sure that the customer gets a consistent experience. The trouble is that the drive for consistency sometimes makes a customer's problem worse instead of better. Here's an example.

> During a visit to a local mobile phone shop Jim saw a phone that he liked instantly and asked the salesperson if he could upgrade his current phone while keeping his existing number. The upgrade was costly so it made more sense to simply get rid of his existing phone and number and open a new account. The salesperson called the mobile phone network and requested that a new account be created for Jim, and his new phone account was up and running ten minutes later.
>
> The salesperson told Jim that he needed to write to the Mobile Phone Company and request that they close his account. 'No problem' Jim thought and went home, new phone in hand, delighted with the simplicity of the transaction and with the speed at which things had been done. That night Jim sat down at his computer and typed the required letter. Near the end of the letter he added a few lines explicitly asking for the mobile phone business not to call him to try and keep his account open. Since he had now opened a new account with them they were not losing a customer at all.
>
> A few days later Jim got a letter from the mobile phone network, telling him they had received his request to close the account and asking if someone could contact him to discuss it. There was an e-mail address provided so Jim sent a polite "thanks but no thanks" reply. Two days after that Jim received a call from a manager at the mobile phone network asking him why he wanted to close his account. At this stage Jim began to get a little annoyed. Jim politely told the manager that he had made all this clear in his letter, and asked her if it was not possible to tell from her computer system that he had just days ago set up a new account. The manager went on to explain that this was the normal process when a customer wants to close an account. The customer is called and an attempt is made to "save" the customer. She went on to ask Jim if anyone else in his family would like to use the account, to which he replied that all of his family were already customers. The call ended with Jim getting his first wish, the account closed, but not getting his second wish to not be contacted.

The people at the mobile phone company surely read Jim's letter but nobody was listening. How can it happen that common sense can be bypassed by an overriding need to stick rigidly to a process? This is a good example of where the very processes put in place to serve customers better and more consistently don't make sense. Sometimes it is consistency itself, the sameness about how things are done, that irritates the customer. Clearly, the customer needs to be more important than the process. The key point here is that by rigidly sticking to a process, those tasked with providing the service slip into a kind of auto-pilot mode, where they stop actively listening and just go through the motions required to provide an adequate level of service. This is not limited to situations over the phone. Some of the most striking examples of businesses not listening to their customers happen in face-to-face situations.

A basic understanding of emotional intelligence reveals that our brains are designed to function through what is known as a limbic connection. This is like a wireless network connecting one human brain with another human brain on a completely sub-conscious level, with no deliberate effort to communicate required. The human brain actually needs these connections with others in order to function as designed. Our facial expressions and eye contact form a big part of this connection, providing the brain with sensory input as we look at the other person. We know intuitively that eye contact and facial expressions are an important part of communication with other people, even though most of us can't fully explain why.

For decades we have known that non-verbal cues and body language have a great bearing on effective communication. The work of Albert Mehrabian[2] in the 1970s and 1980s suggested that cues and body language convey a great deal about feelings and attitude in any communication situation. Clearly an employee hunched over behind a desk not making any attempt to look at his customer is missing out on a huge opportunity to inject some meaning into the communication and into the customer's experience, while revealing a great deal about his attitude to and feelings about the current customer situation. While the person initiating communication carries the responsibility to check that the message is clearly understood we need the other person to respond in kind, either verbally or non-verbally. Difficulty arises when the other person does not want to make contact, does not want to return eye contact, reply to your e-mail, or to even respond to your plaintive shouts of "excuse me".

Sometimes employees don't listen to you because they are fearful of forgetting what they have just spoken to another customer about. For example in a bar or restaurant you may have observed a member of staff visiting a customer's table and taking an order. Often they attempt to memorize the order and then try to get back to the kitchen without forgetting it. As they dash towards the kitchen the only thing they are making eye contact with is the floor. Meanwhile all around customers are trying to catch the employee's eye to place an order.

There is a simple solution that has been tried and tested for decades.

Make sure the employee has a notepad and pen and writes the orders down. While it may look good when employees can remember all of the order or multiple orders it looks very bad when an employee can only remember one order and can't do anything else because they are completely terrified of forgetting that one order. I once overheard a member of staff in a bar explaining to a group of customers how the bar owner told her that she should never write down customer orders because it 'looks unprofessional'. As a customer I don't consider that unprofessional. In restaurants it is the standard method used to guarantee that what you ordered actually gets delivered. Sometimes the order is written down but still becomes mixed up but that's often a case of the wrong thing being written down at the start resulting from poor listening. The idea of deliberately injecting an element of risk into the ordering process is plain stupid. Write it down. We customers won't mind. We won't think less of the employee if they can't memorize an order and have to write it down. If customers are trying to make eye contact with you then look up and look them in the eyes. This is a feedback request from the customer asking "do you see me here?"

Beware the electronic Panacea

It's possible to experience situations where you're sure that nobody is really listening to you when using the telephone. I've also described how this can happen in face-to-face situations. Another cause of complaints is e-mail and social media. There's something mythical about using information technology to provide a form of customer service. Many businesses rushed to get on the Internet, fearful of being left behind as rivals quickly added email and website addresses to their corporate presence. In much the same way that simply having a watering can does not make one an expert gardener, having an email address or Twitter account does not make you an expert in electronic communication with customers. You've got to know what to do with the electronic tool, just like you need to know what to do with the watering can. And that's where so many businesses have missed the point. Offering another channel of communication doesn't automatically improve customer service. Everything depends on who is monitoring communications coming from this new channel and what then is done with them. Here's an example:

> As is the case with most people, Trudi receives a regular supply of junk mail. One of the items she regularly sees is a leaflet from a well-known computer manufacturer informing her about special offers. In all likelihood Trudi is never going to buy one of these computers so she would prefer not to receive these leaflets anymore.
>
> Thankfully the leaflet includes a little instruction at the bottom of the page telling Trudi what to do should she wish not to receive these special offers in

the future. It says simply send an e-mail and the leaflets will no longer be sent.

Trudi sends an email but still receives flyers in the mail. She's now less likely than ever to buy one of their computers. She doesn't bother to send a second request. They didn't listen the first time so why would she believe they will listen now.

If you genuinely want to hear what your customer is saying then you need to listen. If your customer is standing right in front of you then you need to look at your customer and actively listen to what they are saying. If you can't see the customer and they are contacting you in some other way then make sure you do your utmost to listen to what they are telling you through whatever medium they are using to communicate.

Just having an email address, a website with a 'send us a message' facility, a social media account or a fancy telephone system does not equate to listening. It's just a prosthetic ear if it's not genuinely connected to a human inside your business. However, it's not all bad news. I don't believe businesses routinely ignore the wishes of customers because they are rigidly sticking to their own agenda, system, or process. Sometimes things break down simply because the people who receive the communication from the customer simply don't do anything with it, or don't let the customer know what they have done with it. Here is another example to illustrate:

Erik visited a local branch of a nationwide toy store chain to buy a car seat for his nephew. He spent about 10 minutes looking at the various car seats on sale, examining the product information on display and working out what would be the most suitable choice.

A friendly sales assistant approached asking if he needed any help. Erik explained what he was looking for and indicated which seat he deduced to be the best choice. The sales assistant listened and then explained the benefits and limitations of each of the various seats available. She ended up convincing Erik to buy a different seat saving him a great deal of money. It was great advice.

When Erik got home he was so delighted by the way the store assistant had gone out of her way to make sure he made a good choice and didn't waste his money he decided to write to her employer. In his letter he told them that they should be proud to have an employee like this and that they should let her know that she is doing a great job. Erik never received a response from the store.

Is it too much to expect that a store would thank their customer for taking the time to write? Is it too much to expect that a store would let their customer know that the letter made its way to the intended recipient? Clearly it was too much because nobody from the store ever responded to the customer.

Most customers want to be heard. They want an opportunity to discuss something with someone who will listen. When customers contact your business it's not always because they want to complain or whine, even though this is often the way customers are made to feel when they try and make contact with a business.

If you have a website, e-mail address, Facebook account, suggestion box, or even are so bold as to ask people when you meet them for their comments and suggestions, for goodness sake make sure you do something with the information. Don't use one of those awful "auto-response e-mail" systems. So many businesses use them, often to generate a reply that is so fast that you are impressed until you open the email and see that it's from a computer. The only satisfaction you have is knowing that the message made it to the outer layer of the business you are trying to communicate with. Automated systems inadvertently send another message that most businesses don't intend to send, a message that says that businesses don't want you to have the name of a person working there because you might actually call them and want to talk to them. How odd would that really be? Customers in direct communication with employees of your business!

Surely any business that is 100% serious about feedback should have someone monitoring their incoming electronic communications every minute of the working day. So if you provide customers with an email address, your Twitter or Facebook account details, or a 'contact us' form on your website but don't intend to ever read or reply to electronic messages then you're yanking the chain of your customers by offering it under the pretense that you care. Think about how you want customers to contact you with comments and feedback and only implement systems that fit with what you want. If you don't want to receive email or Tweets then don't offer either as a communication channel. If you don't want customers calling in the middle of the night then tell them when you are available to take their calls.

If you have an e-mail, a social media account, or a web-based feedback channel, make sure you put someone competent and responsive working on it and have them acknowledge each and every customer interaction using their own name and using individual messages. If customers feel that, in your eyes, they are just a number then they are most likely right. Customers are human too. When they take the time to contact you, take the time to reply to them right away. Then they might feel like you actually do care. If you tell customers you care then you need to make sure that when they come to tell you something or ask you something, that your ears, eyes and mind are fully attentive to their communication attempts. We all know that hearing is not the same as listening. Listening requires focus and interest.

> Teresa's car phone kit had provided many years of great service. Now it was looking old-fashioned and clunky, with a great big loudspeaker in the dashboard and a cradle bolted onto the side of the dash. When Teresa got her

new mobile phone, the car kit was now obsolete so at her car's next scheduled service, Teresa decided to ask for the car kit to be removed.

On the morning of the service appointment Teresa presented herself at the service counter. The service assistant at the desk asked for her name. She quickly found Teresa's record on the computer and started making preparations for the car to be brought inside the workshop, taking the keys from Teresa. Teresa felt this would be a good moment to ask if the car-kit could be uninstalled. She explained that she wanted the car-kit taken out, and if the garage would kindly dispose of the parts. While Teresa was explaining this, the young lady dealing with her was clearly not listening to what she was saying. She has the distinct sense that the service assistant was thinking "Yeah, yeah. You and your problem. Would you ever shut up?" The service assistant made no eye contact at all, instead looking down or away in any direction except towards Teresa. She also wrote down nothing, not a single word of what Teresa had requested. Teresa feared that maybe she had not been clear in her communication to the service assistant, and tried to explain again. This made no difference whatsoever. Teresa handed over the keys and exited the garage.

When it was time for Teresa to pick up her car, she arrived at the service area and took a seat in the waiting area. Soon Teresa's car arrived out front driven by a mechanic in overalls. He came inside the showroom and handed Teresa's keys to the service assistant at the desk, the same person that had dealt with Teresa earlier that day. The service assistant called Teresa over, printed her service bill and told Teresa that the car kit had been taken out as requested. This made Teresa happy. Teresa paid for the service, took her keys and went outside to collect her car. She unlocked the car and sat in, pleased by the sight of the empty space where the phone cradle used to be. Teresa turned on the engine, pulled out of the car park and drove home. About a half-mile from her house Teresa had a thought. "I wonder what they did with all the parts they took out when they uninstalled the car-kit?" To her dismay, on opening the trunk she found a big useless pile of unwanted car parts. Needless to say Teresa was not happy.

If you don't focus on your customer and don't show real interest in what they are telling you, and don't actively engage so they know you are listening then you'll be just like every other business that pretends it cares. Your customers will know better than that and will eventually gravitate towards someone who that will serve them better and really listens when they have something to say.

PAUSE AND THINK

Don't be lazy when it comes to electronic communications with your customers. Which channels of communication do you currently offer your customer? What is a reasonable expectation for how long a response might take? Who currently works on monitoring and responding to these channels?

Annoying Habit No. 5

Thinking 'good enough' is good enough

Customers often complain that businesses fall short of the standards they expect. Businesses in turn routinely declare themselves willing to give "the extra 1% that will make all the difference". In truth an extra 1% won't make much of a difference to most customers because it's usually an extra 1% of something that the customer does not value or will not notice. Sadly, businesses today tend to compromise on the finer points of service, on the things that actually do matter to customers. Often what is overlooked is something tiny, simple and personal that takes little effort to provide. It drives customers mad when businesses cut corners, leave out important details or make assumptions about what the customer wants or thinks is important. Customers want a job done right. They want businesses to deliver what was promised and they don't want to find nasty little unfinished surprises after the bill is paid. To add an extra 1% that really matters you have to pay careful attention to the detail that your customer is most interested in.

An example:

Charles lives in a house with an old stone wall running along the side of his garden. In recent years the wall has become covered in creeping ivy. Charles and his wife decided that the ivy had to be cut away and though Charles tried cutting it back himself he soon gave up on that idea. It was taking forever. It was time to call in the experts. An entire gardening crew arrived promptly but an hour later their van left, leaving just one gardener behind. It should really have sounded alarm bells in Charles' head when the sole gardener rang the doorbell and said that he didn't have a ladder and needed to borrow one. To his credit, the lone gardener got to work, even continuing during some pretty dreadful rain.

Lunchtime passed and the original gaggle of gardeners returned. At three o'clock in the afternoon they rang the doorbell, stating that the job was done. Charles paid them and they left. When the rain had stopped Charles went to inspect the work more closely. It became clear that they had cut away some but not all of the ivy. They had not done the job properly and now they were gone, cash in hand.

Given the rain, the fact that most of the crew was absent for the day, and the amount of work to be done, the gardener may have mistakenly concluded that his effort was 'good enough'. This mistake in customer service leads to a huge amount of frustration for the customer. A customer might believe that had they been clearer in their instructions the job might have been done better. It is common for customers to feel that a bad job could partly be their fault. In reality most customers are perfectly clear when they explain what work is required. Things often go wrong simply because of poor listening. Additionally a palpable lack of desire to deliver work to the standard that the customer wants is usually a factor too. To deliver a job to the exact specifications of a customer will always take more effort than doing the job to a 'good enough' standard. 'Good enough' has become a paradox when it refers to quality and workmanship. It implies an acceptable standard. The question is who decides what is acceptable? In this case the gardeners decided on the acceptable standard, resulting in what the customer perceived to be the bare minimum of work. In the customer's eyes the garden maintenance firm managed to get paid for doing enough but not a fraction more.

Businesses that aim to survive by doing just enough are creating problems for themselves. There are many examples of businesses that ignore the important details yet somehow manage to survive by stumbling from one annoyed customer to the next, safe in the belief that there are plenty more customers out there.

However, the world suddenly seems like a smaller place now. Customers talk to other customers. Almost every reputable website offering products and services allows users to contribute comments and ratings. In the example above, it's a certain bet that Charles will never recommend that gardening service.

All good businesses know that real success in sales means that it's never about winning the first sale but rather it's about earning repeat sales. In Harvey Mackay's book Swim with the Sharks Without Being Eaten Alive[3] he notes that "little things don't mean a lot. They mean everything". If there are thousands of ways to mess up and annoy your customers then you'll be likely to find them, maybe a few at a time each day. Almost all of these mistakes can be avoided by showing a little more regard and thought for your customers and by paying attention to detail. It's not hard to do the right thing, but it involves hard work to make sure that all the little details are right. Keep looking for little problems, keep searching for annoying errors, and stamp them out. This is how to reach the extra 1% that your customer will really notice and appreciate.

PAUSE AND THINK

Are you sure you fully understand what your customer wants? Does your customer fully understand what you can actually do for them? Aim to set realistic expectations and to always meet them. Pay attention to the little details that could turn out to be really important to the customer.

Annoying Habit No. 6

Staying on your own side of the fence

One of the key differences between businesses that enjoy the positive regard of their customers and those that don't is the way they see their customer's world. Businesses that show customers that they understand the customer's world and can see the customer's view of things have a great chance of keeping their customers and the profit those customers bring. Businesses that don't make much of an effort to see things through their customers' eyes tend to see customers as adversaries. They think customers are always trying to get something for nothing. They see customers as a drain on business profits.

The key to earning the positive regard and loyalty of your best customers is to develop double-vision, or more accurately double-perspective. If you want to serve your customers with excellence and want them to come back time and time again you need to be able to see the world through both your own eyes and those of your customers. In their outstanding book First, Break All the Rules[4] Marcus Buckingham and Curt Coffman emphasize the critical importance of what they term "partnership" when it comes to customer service. They describe partnership as seeing a customer's problem from the same side of the fence as the customer. In other words, instead of adopting adversarial positions, it makes more sense to essentially say "yes, I can see how the problem looks from where you are standing, let's try and solve this problem by attacking it together". This is a really powerful yet obvious insight because it gets right inside the heart of excellent customer service.

If you want to give great service or want to be known for great customer service then you need to see the world from your business's point of view and at the same time from your customer's point of view. This sounds easy to do but it can be tricky.

Truly seeing your customer's point of view is not a simple matter of describing the problem in the customer's terms, or paraphrasing the problem as described by the customer. These skills can help but they are not enough. They are both examples of talking like the customer. You need to start thinking like the customer. This is harder to do because each person has their own highly-developed thinking patterns and processes and these are built-up over years of experience. We think the way we do because experience has led us to believe that it is effective. These thinking patterns, or cognitive frames, are deeply embedded and are hard to change. Because we all have highly-developed ways of thinking that have served us well in life thus far, it rarely crosses our minds to 'step out of ourselves' to see things from the other guy's perspective.

Jay works for a large International IT business. His boss called him in and said that two American customers, Zak and Terry, would be flying in to help get a new project up and running. Zak and Terry would be staying for three months and an apartment in the city had been organised for them. Jay's boss asked him to meet the two new arrivals at the airport and make them feel welcome.

Jay got on the phone with Zak and Terry a few days before they departed and found out that neither had ever spent an extended period of time abroad before. They didn't have much of an idea about what to expect coming to a new country and were both excited and nervous about it. Jay ended the call with them by saying that everything would be arranged and that he'd be waiting for them when they landed.

A few years before Jay had made his first trip overseas on business for a week. Jay remembered walking out of the arrivals hall as a young inexperienced traveller. He remembered the noise, the heat in the air and the strange smells of a new place. He remembered how disorientating it was to land in a new country in a different time zone and understood how hard it can be to find your way around. He remembered that on that day nobody was waiting for him and how vulnerable and nervous he felt at the time. Jay decided that he wanted Zak and Terry to have the best possible experience. He knew it would be important for the two visitors to have a relaxed and straightforward welcome because that would set the tone for their entire time in the country.

On the day of their arrival he made a big colorful sign with the business logo and their names in big letters. He arrived in plenty of time at the airport and waited patiently until he had found a parking space right next to the arrivals building so they wouldn't have to drag their luggage too far. In the arrivals hall he found a great space right in front where he held up his sign and waited. As the two tired visitors emerged into the morning sunshine from the arrivals hall they immediately spotted the sign and made straight for Jay. Their stay was off to a great start.

Of course it helps if you have personally experienced what your customer is experiencing, so you can draw on your own understanding of a situation but it's not essential. Central to the idea of developing the capacity to think what the customer is thinking is the ability to almost step outside of your body and see the situation with neutral eyes. By becoming detached from our own entrenched position, our own biases and our own previous experience of 'customers just like this' we can make progress in helping to move towards the low-stress win-win situation that we all really want. Refusing to see things from the customer's perspective leaves us in ridiculous situations such as customers complaining to staff in restaurants only to be informed "no-one else is complaining".

When a customer calls a waiter over to complain that his food is cold, or that the dish on the table is not what he ordered, or that the temperature in the restaurant is too cold, he's trying to tell you something important about your business. He's trying to tell you that you and your colleagues are doing things that are dissatisfying your customers. No customer actually enjoys making a complaint when they could be enjoying their meal instead. Wake up and listen to what the customer is saying, and try to understand it from their perspective. It could be that your customer is telling you something really important that you definitely need to know.

Naomi enters a fast food restaurant on a really busy day. Restaurant employees are buzzing around behind the counter, plucking fries and burgers from racks and filling up trays at furious speed. Right in the middle of it all there's a dad ordering four kids meals. One child wants a plain hamburger, another wants a cheeseburger with no pickles, and so on. The queues start to slow down and people are hemming and hawing, waiting impatiently to be served. Everyone seems to be looking left and right, wondering if they should have joined a different queue.

Naomi edges slowly towards the counter and is now second in line. Just then a new cash register is opened right next to her. For some reason unknown to her, Naomi must have become invisible because the employee working the register that has just opened calls the person behind Naomi to the counter for service. Surely the employee can see Naomi standing there?

Why do things like this happen? It happens because the person behind the counter is not thinking like their customer on the other side of the counter. They are not connecting with the feeling of injustice and frustration that this kind of action causes in the minds of customers patiently waiting in line.

Al offered to take his brother's car to the garage for a routine service. The garage was very near Al's place of work and he figured he could bring the car to the garage first thing in the morning and then take a taxi to work.

Al arrived at the garage shortly after 8:00 AM only to be told he was in the wrong place. All cars were serviced at a special service location about two miles away. Annoyed, Al got back in the car.

He pulled up in front of the service centre some time around 8:15 AM and found the place locked shut. Shortly afterwards a car pulled up and a man jumped out, removed a lock from the gate, then jumped back in the car and sped away. A woman then arrived and entered the yard of the service centre. It was obvious that she was an employee of the garage so Al stepped out of the car with keys in hand.

"We're not open until eight-thirty" the woman informed him. "I just want to drop off the car for a service" he replied. "You'll have to wait – we're not open yet" was her response. So, Al waited and waited. At 8:30 the woman reappeared and said "Now, what can I do for you?"

In situations like these you have a choice to do the right thing for the customer or do the right thing for yourself. You can choose to keep the customer waiting while you do what you prefer to do but in the back of your mind you already know there will be an irate customer waiting for you when you're finished. Clearly business hours exist for a reason but in this case it's just easier to do the right thing for the customer. No customer wants to waste 10 or 15 minutes sitting in the car park when it's easy for you to take the keys and let them get on with their day. If your main concern is re-educating customers about your opening hours then you're failing to understand your customer's perspective.

When you do have to tell a customer that they have made a mistake, don't act like their stupidity is ruining your life. Just tell them clearly and politely what they need to do. Keep it friendly and fair and it will go a long way. We came across this earlier as Annoying Habit No. 1, 'pointing out that your customer is wrong'.

When a customer arrives at your premises before you are open for business, don't scowl at them and wish they would leave you alone. They could have arrived early for any number of reasons and you can be pretty sure that they wouldn't willingly choose to sit outside doing nothing. Instead of wishing they would get lost why not try a more practical approach. If what they want to do can be done without any real difficulty, such as allowing the customer to drop off their car for service, then why not just do it? If you don't open for a considerable time, why not recommend a nearby coffee shop or better still offer to bring the customer a cup of coffee while they wait.

Every contact with a customer, irrespective of the time of day that it happens, is a moment to create, enhance or damage a relationship. Do the right thing every time and think about the customers' context. Although it may feel like they need you, in reality it's you that needs them.

As humans we tend to harshly judge other people's actions while conveniently and lazily ignoring the possible reasons for those actions. We attribute other people's actions to their personality while we judge our own actions with a full consideration of the context in which our actions take place. This is called the "attribution error", and it plays out vividly in situations where employees take the view that customers do certain things because they are unintelligent or trouble making, all the while ignoring the context and the mitigating circumstances that explain customer behaviour.

Customers notice when you do something thoughtful for them. They notice when you show understanding, flexibility and sensitivity about where they are coming from. When you demonstrate that you understand their perspective, your customers will respect you. If you want your customer to experience great customer service when they come into contact with your business you need to move beyond caring only about yourself, your rules and your needs. Great customer service demands that you send a message loud and clear that you care about your customer. You do this by demonstrating through your words and actions that you understand their perspective.

PAUSE AND THINK

To truly deliver an outstanding customer service experience you must have a deep and real appreciation of their point of view. This requires paying full attention, carefully listening, and starting with a genuine positive regard for your customer.

4 CEMENTING FAILURE: CHANGING FOCUS WHEN YOU GROW

Growth and success are exactly what a small business should strive for. However growth and success bring challenges too. As your customer base expands you might find that your business needs new or additional supervisors, team leaders and managers. You might decide to create new layers or a formal hierarchy of control. You might find that you need more systems, procedures, work manuals and documentation and many other things that up to now were the preserve of big corporations.

It's natural to want to be more organized as your company grows. The danger for small business owners is that you find yourself further and further away from your customers. You lose sight of their needs and how well you are meeting those needs. As businesses grow they spend more and more time looking inwards at brand, metrics, systems and processes. When small businesses grow, even slightly, they can find themselves sucked in to a world of distractions from the core business of serving the customer with excellence every time. The sad fact is, as you become more consumed with your own growth you may lose sight of your customers' needs.

Annoying Habit No. 7

Telling yourself how wonderful you are

It's often surprising to hear businesses proclaim their own greatness, enthusiastically informing their customers about the great service the customer is receiving. Very often what a business says it does for customers is not mirrored by what the customer actually experiences. Businesses are guilty of occasionally exaggerating, claiming or promising to do things because they want to be liked. Often when making these exaggerations, claims or promises businesses know deep down that there is no way they can honor them. This sounds like an integrity issue, but in many cases it's not really integrity that is the problem. Often the problem is self-perception. How businesses see themselves is often completely out of step with how others see them.

> Scott worked part-time as a sales assistant in an electrical store. He had always been interested in electronics and enjoyed fixing up old radios and VCRs. One day while walking through the store's warehouse Scott overheard his boss talking to one of the delivery guys. There was a problem. A customer was expecting delivery of a TV set but they also needed the TV to be set up. The normal TV delivery guy was not available and the one on-duty delivery guy didn't know how to setup a TV. Scott's boss looked at him and said, "You know how to do that, don't you? You know how to setup a TV". Scott nodded and confirmed that he'd be able to do it. So the TV was loaded into the van and Scott jumped in for the 10 minute drive to the customer's home.
> When he arrived there were two elderly ladies waiting impatiently for their new TV set. Scott unpacked the TV from its box, moved the old set to the side of the room, and put the new TV on the table. It took a few minutes but eventually Scott had the new TV set up in exactly the same way as the former TV set. When he was finished Scott stood up feeling pretty pleased with himself for a job well done. Then he noticed the two ladies. They were standing behind Scott, watching him, each with the right hand pressed against her chin. They did not look completely satisfied.
> One said "is that the best you can do?" Scott was amazed by the question. "The picture on the old TV was better than that". Scott knelt down again, checking one more time that he had not missed anything. The truth was that they were looking at the best possible picture from this particular set. He explained that the signal might be weak from their wall socket and that might have a bearing on the quality of the picture. However as he looked at the screen the picture was perfectly normal.
> Scott loaded the old TV into the van and headed back to the warehouse. He was struck by a feeling of disbelief. He thought that what he had done was above the call of duty, thinking how wonderful he was to fix this problem at short notice. It was difficult to accept that the customer just didn't think it was anything special at all. The customer had no idea that this was not part of

Scott's regular duties, and that he was trying to do them a big favor.

Who decides what is special?

The real question is whether it's the business or the customer who defines if a special offer really is special. Sometimes businesses put a lot of effort into setting the scene for customers to enjoy an offer and then slap the customer's hand when they reach for it. Why does this happen?

> There is a mini-supermarket near Silvia's home, which often has big posters on the front windows advertising special offers. Sometimes the special offers involve beer or wine, other times fruit and other food items. The current special offer involves furniture. The idea is simple. When a customer makes a purchase they are issued a collector's card, and each time a customer spends a certain amount the store puts a stamp on the card. When customers have collected a full set of stamps they can bring the card to the store and exchange it for a small piece of collectable furniture, in this case a small table.
>
> Silvia arrived in the store with a fully completed collector's card to exchange it for the table. The employee at the checkout counter explained that there were no more tables in the back of the store but that they would be getting a new delivery in the next couple of days. Silvia was really disappointed. Then she had a brainwave. She pointed at the piece of furniture on display in the store, and asked the employee if she could have that. The employee hesitated. He clearly didn't know what to do. He came out from behind the counter, examined the table, and came back and said that the item might be a little shop soiled. Silvia, clearly excited now, said that this was no problem and that she would take it exactly as it was. He then went on to say that he wouldn't be able to offer her a discount since it had only been on display there for a couple of days. Again Silvia was perfectly happy to accept this.
>
> The manager now appeared from the back of the store. The employee, obviously seeking to do the right thing and gain approval from the manager, asked the manager if it was OK for Silvia to take the display furniture piece in exchange for her collector's card. "No" was the response. "It's not for sale." Now there were two puzzled faces. Silvia looked extremely disappointed while the employee looked embarrassed. Silvia repeated that she did not want any discount and would take the furniture as seen. "Not for sale" repeated the manager. Silvia picked up her handbag and left. The employee stood at the counter, in shock. The manager slinked away into the back of the store.

In summary, the customer wanted the special offer but the store manager told her she couldn't have it. What made this even more annoying for the customer was that the staff member tried to give her the special offer only to have it withdrawn by the manager. And worse again, not only did the store manager refuse the customer what she wanted but he also failed to provide any form of alternative solution or idea for how the customer might be satisfied.

Your customers don't care about your problems. They come to you in the expectation that what you say you can do is valid and can be demonstrated. If you can't do something then don't offer it, and be honest about it up-front. If you explain up-front that you can't do something it sounds and feels like genuine consideration for your customer. Telling your customer after they asked for something that you can't deliver it sounds like an excuse or poor planning on your part.

Never promise something you can't deliver in exactly the way that customers expect it to be delivered. You'll soon get the wrong kind of reputation. Likewise, you can't market a special offer if it can't be realized under normal circumstances. If you take the time to put posters up all around the place proclaiming your magnanimity and your generosity you'd better be sure that you can act it out and match your words.

Judging customers' motives

Marketers would have us believe that every market can be neatly segmented along various lines. In truth these so-called segments are entirely artificial and arbitrary. We know intuitively that there is no single type of buyer for any product on earth any more. Perhaps more than any other, the sales profession is littered with fables about sales people uttering immortal words to prospective buyers like "sir, if you have to ask how much it costs then you clearly can't afford it". Think about the potential damage you might be doing by forming an impression that you and your product is very sophisticated and that it's not appropriate to sell it to certain types of customers. Ultimately, the customer, and only the customer, will decide.

The customer will always decide

Author Harvey Mackay[5] has a great expression for summing up this concept of special offers. He says, "It's not how much it's worth, it's how much people think it's worth". This is a critical point. Fantastic offers have been devised and rolled out from the boardroom. The question is how many of these are actually perceived to be such special offers by customers, especially if the employees between the boardroom and the customer are routinely messing things up. Your customers will decide if a special offer really is something special. One absolute exists in this area: If you attract a customer on the basis of a special offer and then fail to deliver what they expected to get, you will have done a huge amount of damage. They may never come back based on a lousy first experience of your way of doing business.

PAUSE AND THINK

Take a little time to go and speak to real customers. Ask them if they think you're as great as you think you are. Ask an honest question to get some honest feedback. Sometimes hard truths can be the greatest gift you'll ever get as a business.

☐

Annoying Habit No. 8

Investing time and effort in bad practices

Some ideas in business are fantastic. Competitors look at them and ask, "Why didn't we think of that?" Usually, we tend to think in routine and predictable ways. However, when something forces us to look with a new perspective, that's when we can find inspiring and creative ideas. On the other hand, some ideas are lousy and should never make it out of a brainstorming session, yet they do. One such lousy idea is calling prospective customers at home in the evening just as they are about to sit down to dinner. The prospective customer is more than likely to be present and available. This is a safe enough assumption. Most people are home at dinnertime. The real question is whether a prospective customer is likely to be happy about a call from a complete stranger trying to sell him or her something just as they are about to eat dinner.

Clearly you could make the case for a business model built on sheer percentages to justify these calls. If you call enough people and even a small percentage end up buying something from you then you can actually make some money with this approach. However, what kind of customer service experience can you possibly expect to create, what kind of loyalty can you honestly expect when your entire premise for doing business is that you don't care if you annoy the majority of those you contact?

If you are a business owner who cares about keeping the customers you already have then ask yourself whether you would want your best sales person to call an existing and valued customer just as they were about to sit down to dinner and ask for some additional business. Customers would soon get tired of these irritating calls. So why is it that this kind of call is not appropriate for existing customers yet good enough for prospective customers?

The first impression with a prospective customer is the key impression, the moment of truth. This is the point at which most people form a distinct impression about your business and about the person at the other end of the phone. If you are trying to attract customers and capture their interest, maybe it's time to go back to the tried and trusted way. Find a time that's convenient for the customer and prepare properly before you call by finding out all you can about the customer. There is nothing worse than an irrelevant call at an inconvenient time.

Business practices should add value

Every contact with a customer or prospective customer should 'add value' in some way. Businesses should be able to add value by increasing the amount of a something important that a customer values such as money, confidence, free time, health, rest etc. Businesses can also create value by taking something away from a customer, freeing the customer up to do the things they want to spend their time on. For example, childcare is a way of adding value by taking away some of the responsibility of looking after children, providing a parent the opportunity to do something valuable with this freed up time.

If your business does not provide customers with more of something they want or take away something they don't want then you're really not much use to them. Yet we continue to engage in silly business practices that don't add value and waste everyone's time and money.

> Keri's credit card bill is like a narrative on what she has been doing for the last month. On Monday 4th Keri went to the hardware store. On Wednesday 13th she went to the cinema.
>
> With all the information technology used in business these days it's reasonable to expect that these household bills represent an accurate and fair presentation of the services actually used by Keri.
>
> There's something else that intrigues Keri though. Keri always pays her credit card bill using Internet banking. As she reviews her bills she thinks "So they seem to know all about me, where I shop, what days I shop, and how much I spend. So it is reasonable to assume they know how I pay my monthly credit card bill".
>
> Keri wonders why her bank continues to send her a payment envelope with every single credit card bill when she has never in all her time as a customer of the bank used this payment method.

It is odd that a bank can know all about every single store where their customer likes to shop but does not appear to know how their customer pays their credit card bill every month. Business practices that don't make sense are always a waste of their customers' money and that's bad news in any line of business. Businesses continue to be seduced by the idea that spending ever increasing amounts on new computer systems, new automated answering telephone systems, new brochures and new logos, not to mention millions every year wasted on pointless staff re-training, is somehow going to 'add more value' to the customer experience. There is only one way to find out what will add more value.

ASK YOUR CUSTOMER.

They'll soon tell you if your new idea is really just a bad idea and a waste of their money.

PAUSE AND THINK

Recall the last time that that your business came up with an idea for a new product or service. What did you do? Did you have a discussion among yourselves about whether it's good or bad? Did you share and discuss the idea with some customers? If customers won't pay for it or don't see the need for it then find out why. Learn from experience, involve your customers and make your ideas better.

☐

Annoying Habit No. 9

Short-term problem solving

Being able to solve problems is certainly very important when it comes to customer service. Every year businesses devote huge amounts of time and money to train their staff to fix customer problems efficiently and professionally. Most of this training effort is devoted to teaching people to solve the problems that exist. But what about teaching people to solve the problems that don't yet exist?

> After 20 minutes driving around looking for a parking space Mary had finally made it to the department store where the post-Christmas sale was now in full swing. She took the escalator to the lower floor where the glassware and china section was located and headed straight for a long display of various types of glasses. She quickly found the glasses she was hoping would be there and bundled six large tumblers in her arms and brought them quickly to the checkout counter.
>
> "Can you hold these for me? I'll be right back," she said as she darted back to the shelf for the six matching small tumblers. Returning to the counter she carefully placed the six small tumblers alongside the six large tumblers and drew a long breath of relief.
>
> She watched as the checkout assistant wrapped each glass carefully in paper and placed it on the bottom of a large paper bag. Finally with all 12 glasses wrapped and safely in the bag Mary offered her credit card and collected her receipt. Slowly moving away from the counter Mary made her way out to the car park. The only warning she had was the brief sound of paper tearing and then CRASH! Glass fragments were scattered everywhere as Mary stood holding the handles of the bottomless paper bag that no longer held her prized twelve glasses.

It is important to solve the problem you are presented with. That really is absolutely essential. But most of the time it won't be sufficient because often some other problem is waiting to strike. How could Mary have known that the bag would tear? And what about the checkout assistant? Could he have anticipated that the bag might tear under the weight of twelve wrapped glass tumblers? In fact this problem was highly predictable and therefore preventable. All it would have taken was for the checkout assistant to put the first bag containing the tumblers inside a second bag, or perhaps offered the customer a shopping cart to transport the glasses to her car. Either of these options, or better still both options together, would have added no more than a minute or two of delay and the customer would have been more likely to get her purchases home without any damage at all. So why do businesses continue to teach employees to only solve the first problem?

Assumptions about satisfaction

Sometimes the drive to solve only the first problem stems from the way businesses view the service they provide to customers. Often businesses have a self-oriented view of what constitutes customer satisfaction, mistakenly thinking that a problem solved must equal a satisfied customer. Throw in a performance measure such as "first time fix" and you propagate the very kind of short-term problem solving that can really damage the customer service experience. The tendency to view customer issues as a queue that needs clearing means that the most important thing becomes trying to clear the queue. The focus shifts away from making sure each customer issue is comprehensively and accurately dealt with. The obsession that modern businesses have with measurements and statistics has meant that the most important thing is to get faster at clearing queues of issues while the quality of the solution is a secondary consideration at best.

If you don't feel it you can't fix it

Employees today have more training than at any time before. They have tools and systems and processes and controls that are all supposed to lead to better business and a better customer experience. Sadly that rarely tends to be true. In truth only someone who really understands what a customer is experiencing can genuinely help that customer to address their issue. In business it is always easier to deal with another person if you can see the world from their point of view.

In former times many employees spent years and years working in a business and were likely to be customers of their own employer. They had a highly developed understanding of what it meant to be a customer and the kinds of challenges that customers might face when trying to do business with the business. We came across this earlier as annoying habit #6.

Today employees change jobs with great frequency and don't tend to have that same sense of what the customer experience is really like. They can't empathize as easily with customers who encounter problems. It is this lack of experience, this lack of understanding that makes it very difficult to anticipate the problems that are not yet seen. If you want your employees to be able to solve the first problem and then anticipate other problems then you need your employees to start walking in your customers' shoes. Your employees need to be customers too. They need to understand what it means to do business with their own business. They need to listen carefully when friends and family talk about doing business with the business. And they need to feed back the information to the business so that bugs and silly processes can be weeded out.

See the future

One of the ways that really great customer service representatives are different from others is the way in which they can see the future. They have a capacity to briefly imagine that moment when the customer opens the product at home or tries to use the service provided. Great customer service people project forward and imagine what that experience is likely to be. Projecting forward allows top customer service people to ask the question "is that going to be good enough?" and the best will be ruthless in their assessment.

Great customer service is not always about amazing people with the quality of your work and your attention to detail. It is even more important to project forward and envision the moment when the beneficiary of your work experiences it for the first time. Now more than ever it's important to aim for the wow factor every time.

Overcoming a culture of NMP

It clearly is important to see beyond the first problem and that means that employees need to learn to walk a few miles in their customer's shoes. It sounds relatively straightforward but unfortunately most of the time issues extending beyond the first problem are ignored or not imagined. A little self-deceiving voice in an employee's head says "that's nothing to do with me". It's common to find a culture of NMP, Not My Problem in the modern business. This can be pervasive and poisonous and is usually found in businesses where employees have developed a deep dislike of customers, of processes and of any attempts to introduce clear standards of behaviour in front of customers. Some of this culture of NMP can be deeply rooted in individuals and the best course of action may be to take them out of the customer setting and, in extreme cases, get them out of your organisation altogether. People who behave like this can do real damage to your business and it's your duty and responsibility to manage them up to improvement or manage them out of your business.

Many of the people who appear to have a NMP attitude are not deep-rooted in this belief and behaviour. They can be encouraged and guided to change their approach to dealing with customers and solving customer problems. Often all they need are two things: clear boundaries about what they can and cannot do when solving customer problems; and enough delegated authority to do what is right for the business and for the customer within those clear boundaries. You might hear this referred to as empowerment but it's more than that. Encouraging employees to take full responsibility for each customer situation allows them to develop great judgment, to learn through their failures, and to realize that it really is all about what they choose to do with each and every customer. Encouraging employees to take full responsibility stops them from hiding behind rules and policies and encourages employees to show leadership, courage and intelligence. When encouraged to show their full potential your employees will reveal their true capabilities. Some will thrive and some will come to the realization that perhaps they don't fit in the customer service environment.

Use your brain and claim your kudos

If it's simple to fix a potentially serious but unseen problem then go ahead and fix it, but be sure to tell your customer that you noticed it and fixed it. "I noticed you were running a little bit low on oil in your engine so I topped it up for you". If it will take a little longer and may delay the customer, or if it might actually cost the customer some money, then you need to call the customer immediately when you notice a potential problem. Tell them what you have found, give them the options and ask them what they would like you to do. They may tell you to go ahead and fix it, or they may tell you to leave it alone. That's their prerogative. The point is, when you have a chance to over-deliver you need to take it. That's where "wow" moments come from. Don't be afraid to utter what author Robin Sieger[6] often refers to as the nine magic words.

"Sir, can I help you with anything else today?"

Asking your customer if they'd like you to go the extra mile for them can be a real difference maker, just because you took the extra 2.75 seconds (I timed it!) to utter the nine magic words.

It doesn't need to be legendary

When describing fabled customer service it's hard to avoid the story of the customer who came into a Nordstrom store with a defective product. Legend has it that a customer tried to return some tire chains to a Nordstrom store. The employee recognized that the tire chains in question were not sold at Nordstrom but went ahead and refunded the customer from her own wallet despite the customer's receipt being from another store. The employee is reputed to have then gone to the other store on her lunch break and returned the tire chains and reclaimed her own money. While this fable may be apocryphal, there is no doubt that this kind of response is how you win a customer's heart and mind, hopefully convincing them for a lifetime that you will honor your promise of service and satisfaction to them if they will remain loyal. Nordstrom's policy is to always accept returns and while there might be a short-term cost to the business, such as the cost of a new kettle or the cost of new tire chains, it is small compared with the potential benefits earned by retaining its customers.

Sometimes you have to bend the rules to deliver excellent service. Rules exist to keep people honest and to let customers know where they stand. When the rules, or the process, become a stick to beat customers with, there is something wrong.

If, however, your employees are working on the basis that each customer represents a single transaction, then they will focus on adhering rigidly to the process and to making sure that they don't mess up in the eyes of their employer. In business today everything begins and ends with the customer. It's never about only one sale. It's always about the next sale, and the next one after that. You must work to create customers who will come back time and time again. If you can't apply common sense and give your employees enough leeway to do the right thing for your customers when they need it, your customers will go to someone else who can.

PAUSE AND THINK

Are you doing your best at every opportunity to think ahead to problems or complications that could arise? Do you ask yourself how you could either set better expectations for customers so that they don't get a nasty surprise, or what steps could you take now to help avoid or minimize difficulties later for your customer? Remember the extra bag idea to avoid broken glasses. What other 'extra bag' ideas could you come up with to avoid problems that can be avoided?

☐

Key things to remember

Nine annoying habits that drive customers away

1. Pointing out the customer's mistake.
2. Not listening to the customer.
3. Thinking "good enough" is good enough.
4. Staying on your own side of the fence.
5. Acting like you don't care when you really do.
6. Making customers wish they were somewhere else.
7. Telling yourself how wonderful you are.
8. Investing time and effort in bad practices.
9. Short-term problem solving.

PAUSE AND THINK

If I called in on your business today, how many of these would I find in your business?

5 HOME TRUTHS ABOUT YOUR CUSTOMERS

When it comes to customer service, the truth can hurt. Thankfully if you look carefully there are still great examples of customer service. There are people who do an outstanding job of making you feel good about their business, their product or their service. The disappointing thing is that these people are in the minority these days. Most people employed in customer service roles today seem to prefer not to bother and it's a few shining examples that buck the trend.

In day-to-day life we all form judgments about other people. Customer service is no different. Sometimes we make positive judgments about customers, and other times we form negative judgments. Sometimes customer behaviour is a reaction to our own behaviour but we are quick to blame the customer. We view the customer's reaction as confirmation of our pre-judgments about customers. When our behaviour causes a negative customer reaction we create a very unhappy customer service experience. One key step in developing better relationships with your customers is to notice yourself forming these judgments about your customers. Another is to pay attention to how most customers behave under normal circumstances.

So let's look at some simple facts about customers.

1. Customers are intelligent, they are not stupid. They know when they are being lied to. They know when someone is trying to deceive them and they know when someone is just not really that bothered about their problem or need.

2. Customers have feelings. They are not just a nondescript element in the buying process. They are real people. When you treat a customer badly, they will feel hurt and will report the bad experience to others.

3. Customers don't want to fight with you, at least most customers don't want to. Customers will seek harmony, the path of least conflict and will avoid humiliation and embarrassment. Just like you and me they don't want to be made a fool of.

4. Customers have a great sense of honesty and ethics for the most part and will respond to someone who seems to care about them and who has their best interests at heart.

5. Customers like to be right. Why do they like to be right? Because they decided on you, your product, or your business. Nobody likes to admit they made a mistake. This is fundamental to how we think as people. We like to believe that we think and choose carefully, that we make good and balanced choices and that our reasoning is sound. We don't want to hear a sales assistant tell us that we are stupid, wrong or mistaken. We want the people who serve us to tell us that we are correct in our assertions and assumptions and justified in our choices. Even when we are totally wrong we still like to feel vindicated.

6. Customers are reasonable and have a great desire for fairness. If you listen carefully to what they want they will listen carefully to your perspective. Most of the time customers just want you to do what you said you would do.

7. Customers react like anyone would when they are messed about. When customers sense that they won't get fair treatment many will react by digging in. Customers almost always react positively to someone being honest and fair with them.

8. Customers want to be able to come and shop again. Customers want to go into a store and be dealt with by someone polite and friendly. They want to enjoy the experience so that they can come back again. When customers feel poorly treated they won't want to return. Human beings are habitual by design. We like routine and we like going back to things we enjoy, whether it is bars, hotel chains, airlines, or retail stores. Businesses that treat customers badly, that are not friendly and that don't think about "the visit after this visit" are taking a great risk. The world is smaller and more connected than ever before. You can be sure that if you are unique for all the wrong reasons then your former customers will be sure to tell everyone they can to not bother giving you any custom.

9. Customers have done their homework. Customers are often more informed than you may give them credit for. They know what they are talking about. Salespeople can't get away any more with bluffing about products and services. It's not possible to exaggerate or fake your way through a conversation with a customer. Customers can easily go online and compare product features. They can go to a site like Amazon.com where other users have posted reviews of the product. They can go to price comparison websites and they can search the web for reviews, comments, rants, forums and so forth. They will even search while in your premises.

Customers will come informed. Salespeople can no longer get away with making stuff up when customers come into the store. When salespeople don't bother to research what they are selling, customers will know. They will be polite to the salesperson and then leave. Then they'll buy from someone who really does know what they are talking about. Credibility still counts.

Do customers also hold perceptions?

It may be possible that at the very same time that employees are in the back of the store discussing which customer is the biggest jerk, that customers are out in the car park or talking on their mobile phones or online discussing which business is the most infuriating or the least trustworthy. Scandals and sordid tales of corruption in all walks of life have played a part in conditioning us to be a little more suspicious than before. Where previously we might all have viewed a successful local business as the result of many years of hard work and effort, today some might view that same success as somehow shaped by nefarious behaviour and practice.

The purpose of modern marketing, since its evolution, was to stimulate demand, to inform people of choice and to help one maker of a product to differentiate their product from that of a rival. In more recent times marketing has become much more specialized, much more sophisticated and much more subtle. In doing so marketing has moved into a kind of 'manipulation space' with the advertising of toys and fast food directly to very young children, the creation of concepts with a whole array of associated branded merchandise, and the rise of the logo. Marketing is no longer just about informing and educating and even about simple demand generation. Clever advertisements, the cult stories of subliminal messaging, and urban myths about products have caused customers to be suspicious and skeptical. Today marketing is often about creating peer pressure, the fear of being left behind or becoming irrelevant, or the distortion of reality and facts in the relentless pursuit of market share and brand position at almost all costs. With so much of the Internet devoted to analyzing and discussing the influence and tactics employed by businesses, prospective customers are very aware of who is saying what and how trustworthy those messages are.

Do customers trust businesses?

Nowadays it's impossible to do something really bad in business and have it remain a secret for long. Spectacular accounting fraud and criminal business behaviour are routinely in the news. Regular news stories about despicable behaviour by those who lead businesses surely brings about cynicism in the public. An unfortunate association between business and misbehavior is formed subconsciously and can be unleashed on some poor unsuspecting employee who gives out the wrong change by mistake or forgets to take the security tag off a t-shirt that has just been paid for.

Disgraceful revelations of unethical and illegal behaviour by senior people in businesses such as Enron, Parmalat, WorldCom, Arthur Andersen and many more has rocked a society already reeling from the scandalous behaviour of political leaders. The public must contend with the fact that some of the leading organisations in the world have been scandalously dishonest. Worse yet, people have lost their jobs, their careers and their futures due to the actions of a privileged few. All of this has caused the average person to seriously distrust anyone in a position of power.

Add to this a difficult economic climate as the world reels from the fallout of the collapse of financial institutions, triggering a domino-effect across other industries and markets. Never in recent memory has so much focus come upon the actions of those at the top of politics and business as people scramble for answers about who caused all this mess. This, unfortunately, leads to erroneous sweeping generalizations about business. With enough evidence people may start to believe that all businesses are unethical. 'They are all corrupt' may become a widely-held perception after 20 years or more of scandal and abuse of trust.

The right to complain

If people feel that their trust in business leaders or political leaders has been broken, it is likely that this mistrust will remain with them when they come into contact with a business. This has real and serious implications for the employee or manager that happens to deal with them. A customer that mistrusts a business may adopt a defensive or self-protecting aspect when they come into contact with the business. This means that the employee or manager won't need to do much wrong to prove to the customer that their mistrust or suspicion was justified.

Equally, a customer that does not want to be taken advantage of by a business they suspect or mistrust will be more likely to complain when they feel they have not been treated properly. An increased tendency by customers to complain poses a real challenge in the customer service situation. It is particularly a challenge when those working in customer service believe that customers actually enjoy complaining. It is somewhat understandable that employees will wonder what gives customers the right to get on the phone or walk into a store and start making demands. Employees don't like it when customers walk in, email or telephone and start asking for all kinds of things. So why do those who deal with customers feel so threatened by customer complaints?

Inexperience and rushed training

In the past employees were required to know a lot more about their jobs and as a result typically possessed more specialized knowledge and experience. One obvious change that has taken place over time is the declining role of the apprentice or novice. The concept of the apprentice dates back to the late Middle Ages, and the logic of the practice was rooted in the idea that villages and towns would need to renew certain key skills, and that those skills would take time to acquire. Everyone knew who the expert was and, more importantly, everyone knew who the apprentice was in the local area. Only when the master deemed the apprentice to have acquired all the necessary skills would the apprentice cease to be seen as 'learning their trade'.

While the apprentice can still be found in some trades today, especially in parts of Europe, the understanding that an apprentice must take many years to learn a craft, often while earning low wages, means that it has become a rapidly less-attractive career choice for young people. Instead, nowadays, people start a new job and get a small amount of 'training', and before you can say "hold on a second" they are out there working with customers. At some point we have concluded that someone is ready to deal with customers despite having little or no experience. This makes no sense but it is the norm nowadays. Because we operate today on the premise that 'a little training is all that is needed' the problems associated with a lack of depth of knowledge start to manifest very quickly.

For example, imagine a customer walks into a hardware store and they need some wall fixtures for a particular kind of wall. They seek out a member of staff. The member of staff is 20 years of age and has worked in the store for two months. The customer approaches and asks where the wall fixtures are. Will the employee know where the fixtures are and which fixture is most appropriate? Maybe. What happens if he does not know?

The same thing could happen to a customer walking into an electrical store to buy a $5,000 TV from a sales associate that has been selling TVs for just four weeks, or a home networking kit from someone that has never set up such a network, or an investment product from someone who lacks the experience to answer the questions you really want to ask. In these situations the customer can typically spot that the employee does not have the ability to answer the question. This makes the customer indignant.

Businesses have stopped taking the time to let people learn how to do their jobs properly, and have bought into the idea that anyone can do any job with 'a little bit of training'. Customers have already figured out that employees need the required knowledge and expertise in order to be helpful. It's time for businesses to come to the same conclusion.

You can't fake it

Research in the area of facial expressions[7] suggests that in face to face conversation a customer's exact thoughts will be plastered all over their face. The same research suggests that the employee will also be looking at the customer's face and working out what the customer is thinking. When an employee is bluffing their way around a potential customer will likely go into defensive mode and a mini stand-off develops. At this stage it's possible the employee is thinking, "Why is this customer being such an idiot?" while the customer is thinking, "why do I keep coming to this store? These people know nothing".

Let's be clear. Customers do not "enjoy" complaining. It's a myth to suggest they do. Complaining triggers the release of various unpleasant chemicals into the nervous system from the brain. Complaining is not a process designed by nature to be enjoyable. It is a defensive process designed to raise blood pressure, heart beat, breathing rate and adrenaline. Not a good cocktail for a pleasant visit to the local store.

What you do sets the tone. Customers react to your behaviour. If you display competence and a willingness to help them with their needs then customers will be just as kind to you. If you understand this premise you have a real opportunity to do a great job.

Overcoming the existing mindsets

The problem of viewing customers as serial complainers may present itself across your entire staff. There is often a hard-core of veterans in each organisation who take it upon themselves to disseminate all the fabled stories about 'idiot customers'. Left unchecked these stories are like poison. They will reach your new employees and will poison them with antagonism towards your customers. As business owners, managers and experienced customer service employees, you need to control the spread of these stories and the mindset that creates and spreads them. You need to define the mindset you want in your business towards customers. Then you need to cultivate it by bringing in new people who will behave in a way that you want, and by moving out people who will not do what you want. Remember the customer reacts to the way they are treated by your business. As the business owner, the manager or the customer service employee, it's up to you to decide what behaviour you want from your customers. To do this you must shape the behaviour of your employees. By dealing decisively with behaviour that you don't want you can quickly get the behaviour that you do want exhibited by your employees towards your customers.

☐

Key things to remember

- Customers are smart, fair and reasonable people and will respond favorably to professional service.

- Some customers may be wary of you and your business so you will need to establish your bona fides by delivering on your promises.

- While some customers do complain, no one enjoys complaining.

- Your customers can quickly figure out if employees know enough about the products and services, and will likely go elsewhere if employees don't know enough.

- You can't fake what you really think about your customer.

- It takes time and hard work to build up the knowledge and experience to really do a job well. Stop holding on to the idea that anyone can do any job with a little bit of training.

PAUSE AND THINK

What are you doing to create or re-build trust in those who lead and who make the key decisions? What are you doing for your customers to help them build trust in what you do?

6 LAYING THE FOUNDATIONS FOR RECOVERY

Customer service is definitely an easy target. The Internet is full of web pages dedicated to bad customer service while TV shows routinely pick up stories about customers who feel badly treated. Social media has become an open forum for airing grievances about poor customer experiences[8]. But you can't give up on your mission to provide great customer service because you know that nothing else matters nearly as much when it comes to creating a lasting good impression or a loyal customer.

If you are responsible for customer service then you'll have a vested interest in making great customer service a key feature of your business. It's no good just talking about why service is bad. You'll want to know what to do to fix the problem. This section of the book will address that. At this point you have read about the annoying habits and damaging practices that characterize bad customer service today. You may even have been reflecting on some of the perceptions that dog the relationship between customers and those that serve them.

Let's progress now to the "how to make it better" part so you can start fixing things before bad service threatens the very existence of your business.

But first, why are you here?

Before you can start on your path to delivering outstanding customer service, you really must begin with a clear and absolute understanding of why your business exists

. This might sound obvious but bear with me, understanding this point is vital.

Many great businesses grew from very humble beginnings and, in most cases, the founders knew at the outset why the business should exist and what product or service they would provide. They also set out to provide these goods and services better than anyone else. It's no coincidence that these successful businesses had a clear and narrow definition of why they should exist and how they would operate.

There may be lots of other businesses that do something very similar to what you do. Customers may even think that your competitors do exactly what you do. But you have to be clear about what exactly you do, why your business exists and why it should continue to exist. Do you know right now why your business exists and what it is that only your business can do for customers?

When you can explain it clearly to others in simple and uncomplicated language, that's when you will know when you understand it. Explaining your business clearly articulates what your business does, such as "We offer the widest online selection of wines delivered right to your door within 36 hours of ordering." That's the kind of thing that should be written down as a business's core purpose. This purpose is usually blindingly clear to the person who founded the business but may not be to the rest of the employees, especially if the founder is no longer around to explain it to everyone. When done right, the core purpose should be known and felt by everyone. The only way to ensure this is the case is to keep communicating it. But there is a trap.

So many businesses think that using posters, banners, screen savers and e-mails from the boss are all highly effective ways of communicating the core purpose of the business. This approach to communicating the core purpose is doomed to failure. For employees to really understand and recognize the core purpose of a business it must be ever-present in the language of the business. It should be referred to at every available opportunity by anyone who manages people inside the business. Opportunities to remind employees are abundant. Every time someone in a position of responsibility has an opportunity to speak to one or more employees the core purpose should be part of the message. Without a clear reason why your business should continue to operate, there is no mandate to continue. You will follow trends and fads and leave yourself exposed to the vagaries of markets until one day you will cease to serve any useful purpose.

Control comes from clarity, and clarity comes from keeping the message simple and short. If you want to know what people in your organisation do so they can teach others to do it too, then the capacity to be crisp and concise about what your organisation does is critical. If you are not clear about what a job entails, you can't realistically expect your employees to deliver the result you want.

Your concept of right and wrong

Just as important as the purpose, every business needs to figure out what it is not willing to do. It is vital to have a strong sense of right and wrong when it comes to the way business should be conducted. Businesses often get into difficulty when they stray far from what they feel is right. They follow the lure of profitable, but unethical, ways of doing business. Enduring businesses, on the other hand, have a strong sense of ethics and these ethics are usually rooted in the ideology of the person who founded the business. If that person is no longer around then you need to think carefully about what you believe to be the "right way" and the "wrong way" to do business.

It's up to you to define the line that you will refuse to cross when put to the test. Some businesses don't have a line, and when an enticing but illegal opportunity comes along they jump at it. If you genuinely want to have a future in business you've got to have a line that you simply won't cross. To your customers and your suppliers, the line will define what kind of a business you are. Firms that don't or can't agree on a clear set of right and wrong behaviours will do whatever they like, and often things go well for a time. Invariably they end up getting caught in some difficult situation and end up out of business. There is only one way to succeed in business over the long term: you need to be 100% clear why you exist and 100% clear about how you're going to run your business.

At the same time that business leaders are using every available opportunity to remind employees of their purpose, they also need to behave congruently at every moment. You can't last in business if you are meeting customers and promising them 100% professionalism while behind the scenes employees are breaking the rules, behaving unprofessionally and disrespecting your customers.

Determining the behaviour of others

If you have ever tried to impose your will on other people, even for the smallest and seemingly trivial matter, you will have learned that human beings are not designed to blindly follow. This is especially true in situations where people are asked to unilaterally accept rules and ideals that they don't agree with or can't accept.

In the modern business world everyone who is involved with your business has a vested interest in your success. The people who buy from you want you to succeed so they can continue to buy. So do the people who supply you with products and services, your own management team, your employees and so on. As the leader of the business, you can decide what you think should be the purpose of the business and the way you will choose to do business but you will need to share that with your employees and let them comment on it. Share it with customers too, the ones you value and trust and who have a long-standing relationship with you and understand what you stand for. Also, share it with your suppliers. If everyone knows what you are trying to do, and how you want to do it you can create a consistent and harmonious system. There's no reason why this can't help your business.

Harvard's Michael Porter[9] coined the term "The Value Chain" to illustrate the relationships between different parts of a modern business. His wonderfully simple model has been used extensively to show how outside elements (customers and suppliers) link into a business and how inside a business all the various parts link together in sequence until goods or services flow out the opposite end on their way to the customer. Why not set yourself the objective of making sure that every part of your value chain, inside and outside your business, understands your way of doing business and your core purpose. In that way everyone will know where they stand and anyone not willing to play by your rules of how business must be transacted can step away and a more suitable supplier or customer can be found.

Profile the work

It is crucially important in every business to have the right people with the right skills and experience in the right roles. Doing so means you give your business the best possible chance of success. Equally important is getting the wrong people out of the wrong roles or out of the business altogether. This is both drastic and vital. It is also hard to do. Telling someone who is ineffective but comfortable in their position that they just don't belong there is fraught with danger and all kinds of painful interpersonal difficulty. However before you start examining your organisation chart looking for people who don't fit, you need to think carefully about what you are about to do.

How clear are you about your business and what is does? After reflecting on why your business exists you should be able to clearly state the core purpose of your business. How clear then are you about what the people who work for you need to do? How well can you profile the work that a particular employee should do? A lack of clarity about what the job involves is where a huge percentage of 'people problems' begin. Amazingly, the typical employee in a business today struggles to understand what is expected of them when they come to work. Sometimes this happens because managers don't communicate what is expected. Other times it's because what is communicated is poorly explained or too complicated. To lead people effectively you need to be able to communicate with absolute clarity. You have to be able to articulate your plans and intentions with such simplicity that every employee understands what you are saying the first time they hear it. Very few of today's businesses have managed successfully to inform their employees from top to bottom about what is critical for them to do.

It takes time to communicate what is important. Sometimes it is tempting to leave this job to someone else. Sadly many businesses continue to adopt the "watch Frank" strategy. This is where an employee shows up for work on day one of his new job. The boss meets him and introduces him to Frank. The sum total of the guidance given to the new employee is as follows. "This is Frank. I want you to stick next to him today and watch what he does. You'll be doing it by yourself tomorrow". What happens if Frank doesn't care about your business? What happens if Frank doesn't care about your customers and certainly doesn't care about your new employee? What if Frank has his own values and has his own deeply ingrained view of what is right and wrong about doing business? Do you want to trust Frank with your new employee? A startling number of employers do. Is this the kind of clarity and the sort of start you want your new employees to experience?

Assumptions, presumptions and actual expectations

A startling number of businesses stray away from developing a clear and simple understanding of what they should be doing and instead blindly chase after today's mantra of 'adding more value'. This tends to result in businesses adding ever more services and features for customers with scant regard for whether customers really value them at all. In truth, customers in many cases don't even notice that you're doing all this extra work in the name of adding value and they likely don't care.

Research shows that service quality is overwhelmingly determined by customer expectations. So when a business's understanding of those expectations does not match actual customer expectations the customer's perception of the service quality will worsen. Continuing research in this area suggests that often customer expectations of service are nowhere near as high as businesses believe them to be. Businesses often mistakenly think that customers will demand services A to Z when in truth customers will be perfectly satisfied with services A to D. This is of fundamental importance as you set off on your journey to distinguish yourself from your competition. With the aim of creating the most satisfied customers in the market the biggest mistake you can make is to think you and your staff know what customers want. The only way you'll really know what customers expect you to deliver is by asking them. And then asking them again. And again. And again.

Assumptions and presumptions are like dynamite to a business. They have the potential to destroy your capacity to focus on what you should be doing. Once you know what you should be doing make sure you can get that message clearly delivered to each and every person. It is the one thing they need to know about what your business is trying to do.

And finally, if you really want to know what it's like for your customers to do business with you, step into their shoes and experience it for yourself. Pick up the phone, go online or walk into a store where your organisation does business and see how satisfying the experience is. Wal-Mart founder Sam Walton[10] used to routinely do this by visiting his stores around the US. The top team at Toyota Motor are encouraged to exercise genchi genbutsu[11], which translates loosely to mean "go and see the problem for yourself". When you have learned what it feels like to be your customer, and when you have asked your customers what they expect, you'll be at the point where you know what you need all your people to do and you can get busy doing it. Now you can tell your employee the one thing they should be focused on doing when they come to work.

It's all about the people

Customer service is often described as a mix of components, blending people with processes and systems for a consistent and seamless experience. What rubbish! No amount of great systems or processes or training or leadership or incentives or threats will be sufficient to drive an excellent customer service experience. Customer service, when it comes down to it, is all about what happens between your organisation's representative and your customer. It's all about behaviour. Customer service is all about what your representative does in front of, over the phone or via the Internet with your customer. The person fulfilling this responsibility is of such critical importance that, put simply, if you mess up when selecting the people who will represent you and your business then you risk everything.

While this should not be breaking news to anyone involved in customer service it is, in fact, at odds with the way many customer service staff are attracted and recruited into businesses. You should look with fresh eyes at your employees and ask if you really have the right people working directly with your customers. If your review suggests that you don't have the best possible people in every customer service role then you should think about bringing in new people to fulfill these critical responsibilities. If you are planning on bringing new people into your business, or need to simply replace a person here and there who has left, you need to be really, really particular.

Be wary of what they claim they can do

One classic mistake is to recruit new people based on what they have in their CV or résumé. Most potential hires nowadays can do a really convincing interview. They can make you feel good about them and their capabilities and make you want to hire them then and there. But sometimes it happens that the person who did a great interview turns out to be very different when they are in the job, or when their employee probation period ends. Unfortunately this is very common. If you want to make great choices every time you hire someone new, you need to think differently about how you hire. Finding, hiring and keeping the right people for your business means you need to pay attention to the following key actions:

Focus on the really valuable information

These days a résumé or CV has little or no meaningful value because it is so difficult to prove whether the information is factual, embellished or false. When someone sends you a CV, use it to get an idea of what they choose to tell you about themselves but don't base your decision to hire on a magnificent résumé alone.

Realize that success in the position you're trying to fill will be a combination of the right skills, the right knowledge and the right attitude. You can certainly train people in the job so that they have the right skills. You can certainly help people in the job to acquire the knowledge they need. What about the attitude? Unfortunately most bad hires happen because there is a mismatch between aptitude and attitude. Think about it. During the interview the candidate is likely to tell you anything they think will make you want to hire them. Their attitude will be presented to you as balanced, positive, and enthusiastic. So how do you find out what they are really like?

Successful interviewers delve into an applicant's work history by asking questions about their past experience. Specifically you should look for details on the way they approached key responsibilities and situations in the past. Most interviews fail to deliver good quality information because time is wasted talking about the future and what might be. It's tempting to believe that this is really valuable insight but in practice it is of no value at all to you. Current research suggests that the most accurate predictor of what a person will do in a future job situation is determined by what they did in similar situations in the past. If you want to find out what the person sitting in front of you will do when a customer complains, the most accurate answer will come from asking them to step you through what they did the last few times this actually happened to them. If you can find out how an applicant repeatedly has done something in the past you'll have a decent chance of predicting what they will do in the same situation in your business. What's more, in describing how they dealt with those situations in the past they will reveal not only the skills they used and the knowledge they possess but also their attitude to customers and complaints.

To know what to ask in an interview consider the information provided earlier in this chapter. If you managed to profile the job so that you understand the key elements of what an employee in a particular role should spend their day doing, then you will have the list of situations you need to test.

Let me give an example.

You have profiled a job role for which you have a current vacancy. For the purposes of illustration, let's assume the role on offer is delivering flowers. You have looked hard at what people in the job do all day and you now understand that the job entails the following five main activities.

A. Answering the phone to customers and helping them to get information on what kinds of flowers are available and to which areas you deliver.
B. Taking customer orders over the phone.
C. Processing credit card payments using the IT system.
D. Loading orders onto the delivery schedule.
E. Providing post-sale support to customers such as complaints, missed deliveries, broken flowers etc.

You are about to interview three people for the vacancy to assess if they can do the five things above. That's the sole purpose of the interview. Remember you are not there to get to know them or to help them further their careers. You're holding the interview because you need to hire someone who can do the job the way you want it done. Your future depends on you making a good decision.

First you need to think about what kind of skills a person needs to be able to do item A in the list above. In truth you're looking for a person who is comfortable dealing with customers on the phone. They might have to deal with high volumes of calls at certain times such as Valentine's Day. So you will need to check that they can cope with high volumes of work. You also need someone who is willing to work with repetitive tasks too since many orders will be the same. So in practice for this point you should be asking a question like:

"Tell me about a situation in the recent past where you had to deal with a large number of customers on the phone?"

If they have done this kind of thing before the person you are interviewing should be quickly able to identify a couple of strong examples of situations from their past. Listening carefully to what they are describing you can then ask further questions to test the depth and validity of what they are describing. You are looking for evidence that confirms that they do or don't have the required experience. Clearly if they have never done this before over the phone then it's useful to know if they have ever handled a high volume of customer queries in a face to face situation. If they have not worked in a high volume situation then you need to know what exactly they have done. This might be your first clue that they are not suitable and it could be that they simply don't have the experience of doing what you need them to be able to do. If they come up with a good example, you need to ask them to step you through how they managed to handle the volume of work. They should be describing the systems they used, and in doing so they should reveal some of the knowledge they acquired and their degree of control and composure and the attitude they applied to their workload. Can you see how this works?

You need to be able to clearly identify the responsibilities that you know will be required. You ask them to tell you how they carried out similar responsibilities in their previous roles. You need to question in depth until you're satisfied that they have done it before and that they have consistently done it in a way that fits with how you want it done in the future. There's no point in interviewing any other way than selecting people who have proven experience or proven ability. There are plenty of people looking for work but not many that might perfectly fit the profile of any given job. This process and level of consideration will then need to be applied to all four other aspects of the job.

Continuously scan for great potential

Have you ever had a conversation with an employee in someone else's business and been immediately struck by their obvious talent? Perhaps the thought crept into your mind that the employee's talents were wasted in their current role. Perhaps you have been waited on in a restaurant by someone that immediately struck you as the kind of person you need in your business. If we assume, and it's a safe enough assumption, that the vast majority of businesses have poor hiring practices, it is likely that most businesses have people working there who should not be working there. Chances are high that some of those employees would be happier working for you.

I'm not saying you should poach people left, right, and centre from other businesses. What I am saying is when you meet someone that you really think might be perfect for a job in your business why not invite them to come around and see you on their day off? Have a chat, get them to talk about what they do and how they do it and you're going to know pretty quickly if you should be interviewing them for a job. If you spot talent, approach the person and talk with them for a couple of minutes. It's the least you can do and your customers will thank you for being ever-vigilant and being constantly on the lookout for the best people for your own business. It's not illegal to have a conversation and nowadays the jobs market is a lot more fluid than before.

If every business was smart they too would be looking for only the right people for their business. The fact is that businesses are not smart about how or whom they hire so in reality there are millions of people in the wrong jobs all over the planet. Use your head and when you spot someone who might be a perfect fit for your business go and talk to them.

Tap into the value of proven experience

We often use the words "fresh" and "talent" in the same sentence when it comes to talking about employees. "Raw" is another word we often find paired with talent. This is a common mistake in business, that somehow only the new younger employees will bring new ideas and fresh thinking to your jaded way of doing things. I disagree with this view. The world is heading for a workforce crisis in most of the world's developed economies.

The talent you're missing may not be young, fresh or raw at all. Large numbers of people from their forties to their nineties are available for work and know how to work. You may be making assumptions about what many of these people desire from their work life. Many seek short working weeks. They may not crave promotions and job enrichment the way younger employees do. Often they may seek work for a social connection, to meet people and to provide a focus for their week. They won't likely want or expect to become the next CEO or to break all sales records.

So many businesses are blind to this huge pool of talent in virtually every country. These people may be just what you need in a new employee. So be prepared to look beyond conventional wisdom about where talent is found. Earlier I suggested you should seek employees with proven experience. That doesn't have to mean a 25 year old who has worked in a similar role for three years. It could mean a 60 year old who worked in a similar role for 20 years. Only a fool would ignore this talent.

Key things to remember

- You can't provide great customer service if you don't know why your business exists.

- Your reputation for great service depends on a track record of doing the right thing.

- Great service requires every employee to know exactly what he or she must do.

- Only those who really care about your customers will fit in your organisation.

- Walking a mile in your customers' shoes can be very revealing.

- Never hire on promise alone, hire based on fit and experience.

- There's always room for one more exceptional person in your team.

PAUSE AND THINK

How do you find and select employees? What criteria do you use when selecting them? How clear are you about what the business does and what employees must do? Have you practiced Genchi Genbutsu lately?

7 THE RIGHT EMPLOYEES AND THE RIGHT MANAGEMENT

At this point you should be clear about why you are in business, what exactly your employees need to do in their roles, how you want the work to be done, and who exactly will do the work. Now you need to work out who will manage the people doing the work.

People managers are critical to the success of your organisation because they keep the employees focused on their core jobs and stop them from getting distracted. People managers are key to ensuring that your best people continue to be your best people through the use of rewards, motivational approaches and tried and trusted people skills. Your people managers are responsible for making sure that unsatisfactory performance is not tolerated. Your people managers have the responsibility for ensuring that consistently poor performers either make the required improvement or are managed out of the business.

I'm not advocating that you immediately start firing people in order to get your customer service reputation to where it should be. What I am advocating is that you make sure you have some great managers on board, managers who can help you to work out if any of the low performers could be turned into good or great performers. Employees with potential to change should be saved. If, on the other hand, after a fair bit of cajoling and second chances you realize that some of your people are simply looking to get a free ride courtesy of your business then you need to act. Use your people managers to carefully manage non-performing employees out of the business.

Be careful because employment law can be a minefield, especially if you don't know your way around. Get some good HR advice and don't delay. You will likely find that you need to develop a fair and specific plan for how the person must improve their performance over a given time period. You should do all you can to avoid ambiguity, misunderstanding, or differing interpretation of facts between you and your employee. You need to arrive at a point where you and the employee both accept that you gave it one heck of a go but they are just not ever going to be able to deliver the kind of sustained performance with the kind of high quality results that you need.

If your employee does manage to change and starts delivering great performance on a regular basis then you've hit the jackpot. It's like getting a new employee but without the hiring costs. If they don't change and can't deliver the performance you need over a sustained period of time, then it's better for you both that the employee leaves the business. By now it's well understood that people have the greatest chance of success in life if they do the thing they are naturally good at. So these folks have found out at your expense one of the things they are not good at. You have helped them enough by now. They need to move on and so do you. Don't let the same mistake happen again. Hire systematically and carefully and learn from your mistakes.

Be sure to hire really great people managers using the same principles as before. Hire people managers who can prove that they can do what you need them to do as second nature. Be on the lookout for actors, bluffers and hoaxers and steer well clear of them. They will destroy your business. Hiring mistakes can be catastrophic. They may not hurt right away but when time passes and things get worse you're going to be sorry you didn't pay attention at the start.

Use the managerial network to protect your business

One of the things that I have observed over the years is how we sometimes miss big opportunities when we rely too much on technology. We miss what is right in front of us. We become so dependent on email and other information sharing technologies to keep us up to date with changes that we often neglect informal conversations. It is often through these informal conversations that managers learn of unhappy employees or damaged relationships inside the business. Our desire to protect ourselves in our daily roles means will almost never share information like this through electronic systems. An over-reliance on technology means we have stopped using the best available channel of information on employees in favor of using more formal channels. I have witnessed at first hand great people leaving a business because they didn't like their job or couldn't work any longer with a particular manager or co-worker. What made their leaving more difficult was the fact that other managers would have instantly and gratefully taken that person into their group if it had been more widely known that the person was unhappy and looking for a change. This is sad. Businesses that allow good people to leave are really missing out.

Human beings by their nature have a strong preference for stability. Maslow's pyramid of needs[12] shows that the need for security is paramount. Put simply most people don't want to leave a job. So why don't businesses do a better job of retaining their people by moving them around to other more suitable or more challenging roles?

One theory is that business owners and managers don't care. I've heard it said on many occasions that employee turnover is good for a business because it brings in fresh talent. If you describe the "benefit" in other terms it's not positive at all. For example if you said "Turnover is good because it means we can bring in lower-cost and less-experienced people and hopefully they might work out" would you feel as comfortable? When your best people are leaving there is no good way to rationalize the situation. Naturally if low performers leave you can probably live with that. However research in this area suggests that low performers might be the last people who will leave your organisation, especially if poor performance over a prolonged period of time has been tolerated.

We have become very in the way we manage people, preferring to group people for simplicity or efficiency into neat little groups organized by roles. Businesses are often reluctant to consider moving people on a case by case basis into different roles in order to find the right fit. We are fearful that this kind of personalized action and considered judgment will open the floodgates to all kinds of demands. And what exactly is so wrong with that? Individuals and their managers should work out where the best place is for an employee's talent. How can that be a bad thing? Could it be that we are afraid of the paperwork and processes involved in moving a person that we decide the effort is simply not worth it? Could bureaucratic laziness and a desire for the easy life be really what stops us having the right people in the right roles?

The truth is that we now rely heavily on e-mail, electronic systems and voice mail to make contact with one another. Paranoid about leaving a paper trail that might be damaging in the future, even when there is nothing to fear, managers are loathe to commit ideas and suggestions to writing. So this leaves us with the only option, which is actually the best option: talking with one another.

If it's the best option then why don't we do it? It's difficult to suggest a single reason but it's clear that managers are out of practice speaking to each other in this direct way. While managers are encouraged to carve a career path for themselves this has created the unfortunate consequence that colleagues are now looked on as competitors for future roles or promotion. This does not encourage mutually supportive behaviour and certainly does not encourage one manager to seek out what is in the best interests of another manager or of the wider business.

This could be at the heart of why great people leave. Great employees could just be wondering why a business of outstanding and intelligent people can't find some way to accommodate a good and loyal employee by finding a role that is a better fit or challenge than the role they currently have.

Key things to remember

- Great managers and great management practices will make business thrive.

- Protect what you have worked hard to build.

PAUSE AND THINK

How much focus do you put on the way your managers manage your most precious resource, your people? How hard do you fight to keep great people when they are thinking of leaving?

8 IDENTIFY WHAT IS CRITICALLY IMPORTANT

One thing that consistently amazes me is how poorly modern businesses prepare their employees for work. While almost all businesses teach employees about the business (what the business does, the products it sells, how it provides support to customers etc.) very few businesses seem to take any time to teach employees about its customers. Employees are rarely educated about how customers typically behave and how they react to what the business does. Employees are routinely thrust in front of customers without really understanding what customers want or need and without a proper understanding of what will be required to make the customers satisfied with the service.

Businesses tend to mistakenly chase after the notion of customer satisfaction without a full appreciation of what exactly makes for a satisfied customer. As far back as the 1950s, psychologist and academic Frederick Herzberg[13] was educating anyone who would listen about the fundamental principles that motivate human beings in the workplace. His work set out a basic premise for the factors that impact employee job satisfaction. Interestingly, his work suggests addressing job dissatisfaction does not have much impact on job satisfaction. Businesses fail to recognize this simple truth. Fixing some small thing that is making an employee unhappy in their role will not automatically make them happy. All it does is make them not unhappy. This might sound like semantics but it is a very important point. This has profound implications for customer service because it implies that addressing the causes of customer dissatisfaction won't suddenly lead to satisfied customers. The causes of customer dissatisfaction and satisfaction are very different and are not properly understood by businesses today.

Second, and perhaps more telling, businesses can't afford to generalize about what all customers are like and what all customers want. Sadly this is exactly what businesses tend to do. If you want your staff to do a better job of serving your customers then you need to educate your staff about what customers are really like, how they behave, and what they want. If you don't teach your staff this key information then they will improvise with their colleagues and make it up for themselves.

How important are your IT systems?

It's a perpetual source of curiosity that for all the investment in information technology by businesses in recent decades, there is precious little hard evidence of any meaningful and lasting benefit to businesses or their customers. This is amazing. It's difficult to pinpoint exactly why such investments in information technology appear to be a waste of time. On one side there is definitely an argument that poor implementation is a cause of lost value. Implementation of information technology falls down when the nature of the project changes routinely over the lifetime of the project. This is usually referred to as "scope creep" and is akin to "moving the goalposts" in the middle of a project. This causes all those involved in the project to ultimately develop the feeling that the project is creeping towards eventual failure.

Another cause of implementation failure is lack of clarity. Quite simply those involved in the project do not share a common agreement on what the project is trying to achieve. Slight differences in understanding, coupled with political pressures between functional units involved in the project, eventually causes divergence of effort. The project is left hanging together by threads. These two causes of failure represent examples of problems before (clarity of purpose) and during (scope creep) the implementation.

It could be further argued that significant problems with information technology projects are caused after implementation. Once the new information technology is installed and made available to employees real problems can occur.

Start with the why

Often businesses view significant investment in technology as the key to creating or sustaining competitive advantage. Realizing any kind of advantage from information technology is dependent on who will use the technology and whether they actually can use it effectively. If you are going to make an investment in an IT system make sure that you don't waste your investment by failing to help people to use the system properly. Let's be really careful here: I'm not talking solely about running training classes to show the users how to use the system. You clearly do need to do that's not where the training ends. You need to go much further.

First, you need the users inside your business to understand why you are installing this new system. This does not mean selling the benefits of the new system to the staff. That will come out naturally over the course of time. Rather, you need to define for your staff what problems exist with the previous system and how that threatens the business's attempts to improve and make progress in the market. You need the staff and the users to understand why it has been imperative to change to a new system. If the users can't relate to the rationale for using the new system and simply choose to keep using the old system then there is no real chance of success. Your only option in this case will be to force the users to use the new system against their will and judgment. Sadly most firms concentrate on explaining to users how to use the system, often with no real and meaningful explanation of why a new system is needed.

Chris Argyris, writing in 1991 for the Harvard Business Review[14], illustrated this concept beautifully. He refers to the concept of cognitive reasoning and explains why it is that sometimes the smartest people have difficulty learning. He suggests that most training is set up to explain what to do but fails to explain why. Understanding why, or what Argyris calls cognitive reasoning, is crucial. When we understand why it is important to learn something we can then proceed and learn how to do it. Argyris explains this as having the space to think things through, suggesting that when learners have time to rationalize an idea, they have a much better chance of learning the information accompanying that idea.

If you want people to adopt your new information technology system, you have to help them to first understand why the new system is needed, specifically spelling out what problem or issue inside the business it will address. Then give them a little time to think it over, discuss it with one another, and can reason it out. Once they have had a chance to do that, they are ready to learn how to use it.

Let me give an example to illustrate.

Dan called a hotel to enquire about making a dinner reservation. An employee at the reception desk who was clearly not a native English speaker answered the phone.

Dan asked to be transferred to the restaurant but instead was transferred to the bar. Another employee who clearly didn't understand him when he asked if he had been put through to the restaurant then answered the phone. This employee offered to transfer Dan. Dan then heard a few tones and then heard the phone hang up.

Is it possible that each or all of these employees had been shown how to use the telephone system? Absolutely. Is it possible that these employees did not appreciate the cost of losing customers when customers are mishandled using the telephone system? Yes again. To repeat the point, if you are going to allow your employees to answer the phone to your customers, you need to make sure that they understand why you have a sophisticated phone system and then how to actually operate it. If you give your employees access to excellent tools, make sure they know why you have in these tools and how to use them.

Handling complaints with intelligence

One of the toughest places on earth to be is the other side of the desk when a customer is complaining. Customers don't like to complain. It goes against human physiology and chemistry. Complaining brings stress, anxiety and all kinds of nasty chemicals into the nervous system for both parties in a complaint situation. So, if you have any hunch whatsoever that anyone likes complaining, you need to drop that idea right now. It's simply not true.

Complaining can often be viewed by members of staff as an unwarranted and unreasonable attack on the business. Complaining could be viewed by customers as a right and an entitlement. Instead I'd suggest that making a complaint is an option of last resort. By nature, human beings are relatively patient and generally compassionate. Our evolution has been from unsophisticated thinker to sophisticated thinker. Our emotions have developed in parallel, evolving from reactive to contemplative. In short we have the capacity to think things through to arrive at a good outcome. So, when a complaint situation arises, in most cases the person complaining has had plenty of time to think the problem through and is likely to feel that this is the last resort available to them.

A high level of complaints is bad for business. Businesses should not create situations where customers feel they must complain but, alas, it happens. How you deal with complaints may make or break your business, but it may well make or break your staff. When you have gone to great lengths to attract the right people into the right jobs it makes no sense to expose your best employees to unnecessary stress and anxiety. If the way you do business is the reason for your high level of complaints then you shouldn't be surprised when your best employees decide to quit.

Being prepared for trouble

How you instruct your staff to deal with complaints sends a crucial message to staff about how much support they can expect when things get tough. It would be madness to send a soldier into combat without sufficient equipment or protection so why should an employee be prepared to handle a complaint situation feeling vulnerable and unprotected?

An example in two parts will show how this can go terribly wrong.

Bea was shopping in a local supermarket. At the checkout she had to reprimand the checkout assistant. The assistant had scanned a cake in a box but had then placed the cake upside down on the conveyor belt.

This clearly annoyed Bea, presumably worried that the cake would be damaged or somehow less presentable to her guests after being placed upside down. Bea remained calm and said something along the lines of "you shouldn't have put my cake upside down like that" to the checkout assistant. Here was a moment of truth. How did the checkout assistant react? What did she say? What did she do?

Precisely nothing. Her face was a picture of panic. She muttered something incoherent, maybe "what?" or "eh?" but that was the sum total of her response.

In his book Games People Play[15] Dr. Eric Berne sets out the concept of Transactional Analysis (TA). Dr. Berne reveals some of the psychology behind person to person interactions and suggests that each of us interacts with others through the use of one of three ego states: child, parent, or adult. His concept is that the ego states vary depending on whom we are interacting with or on the situation in which we find ourselves. We switch between these states constantly and each state can be appropriate in the right situation.

Clearly being in the wrong ego state in a given situation is a recipe for difficulty with another person. The most productive interactions typically take place at an adult to adult level, irrespective of the age of the two participants in the situation. This is where reasoned dialogue takes place. Let's go back to the checkout story and see what unfolded.

Bea had now entered the parent ego state and had started lecturing the checkout assistant, who was becoming increasingly uncomfortable with the situation. Bea started telling the assistant how she should learn some manners, then proceeded to tell her how she pays her wages and so on.

At this stage, the checkout assistant was now visibly trembling. She was in the child ego state and was completely overwhelmed by this parental figure lecturing her. She wanted desperately to hide somewhere but there were goods to be scanned. She was trapped.

Bea asked the checkout assistant for her name. The checkout assistant then made a fatal mistake and asked the customer why she wanted to know her name further angering Bea and causing the checkout assistant to shake fear.

Bea paid for her shopping and exited the checkout line. She stopped at an adjoining line and asked another employee for the name of the assistant who had just served her, intent on making a formal complaint to the supermarket manager.

This all went wrong from the moment that the member of staff did not spot the "potential for complaint". The unfolding situation was not foreseen. A simple solution would have been to offer a replacement cake, and to offer to go and fetch it at the precise moment where it was clear that the customer was not happy about the cake being turned upside down. The key here is not to fixate on right and wrong and who said what. The key is to recognize that complaints about service begin with little issues. Dealing with the little issues while they are still little is easier and far less costly. But how do you spot little issues? This is the critical question to answer as businesses train their employees. It all begins with the little stuff, the attention to detail, the critical 1%.

Spot potential problems early and address them quickly, decisively and keep going up to the point where the customer is telling you "Yes, that would make me happy. Thanks!" We'll return to the idea of spotting little issues later.

Do your employees know what annoys customers?

Installing new information systems can help your business but alone they are not enough. It's your job to make sure that employees know how to use the tools of the job.

Like true leadership, fantastic customer service is rarely observed in times when everything is going well. The best measure of customer service is what happens in a moment where emotions are raised and you can seize or squander the opportunity. Most customer service stories begin at such a place, where a customer is unhappy about something and an employee has a moment to decide what to do. Helping employees to spot these potential flashpoints, and to manage their own emotions and those of the customer, lies at the heart of great customer service. Sadly these customer flashpoints are not entirely random. Many flashpoints could be avoided if business owners and managers realized that their business practices are often the cause of these flashpoints.

In a remarkably obvious way, it would therefore be valuable to educate your employees about the things they do that really annoy customers. Customers are often driven to distraction by something that they routinely experience with your employees, often with the employee just following the business policy.

Here are a few examples of things that employees routinely do that drive customers crazy. Identify the particular things your business may do that annoy your customers. Share this list with all your employees for a more peaceful experience for your customers and a valuable tool for your employees next time they discover a flashpoint.

1. Have rules that are not honored

I visited a large hardware store recently. My trolley was full of items for a home improvement job. The store was busy and there were very long lines at the checkouts. This was not the first time I had been to this particular store; in fact I had been here many times before. I happened to remember from previous visits that I had often been able to pay for items at the customer service desk when I had a small number of purchases, saving me from spending ages in the long lines. I wandered over to the customer service desk. This time something was different. There on the counter was a large sign stating "no payments accepted at this desk."

Disappointed, I trudged back towards the now even-longer lines and joined one. Five minutes passed and the line had not moved an inch. Suddenly the staff started calling people to the customer service desk to pay for their goods.

Naturally trolleys everywhere were now sprinting for the customer service desk and I missed the window of opportunity.

If you have a policy then you need to stick with it. If your policy is not adhered to, for example at peak times then for heaven's sake change the policy so that it reflects what you actually do.

It is impossible to overstate the importance of accuracy to your customers. Think of all those times the waiter asked you how you would like your steak cooked and irrespective of what you said the thing was incinerated when it was put in front of you. How many times have you called one of those 24/7 emergency lines for a plumber or a tire repair only to get voicemail or someone saying "I won't be able to get over to you before tomorrow morning"? Accuracy. It's primal. Customers don't want it. They demand it. They certainly expect it. When you say you're going to do something then you better do what you say. This is so obvious yet so few businesses deliver on what they promise.

2. Offer something that can't be delivered

Standing in line one day, waiting to be served at a "gourmet" sandwich counter, I overheard someone trying to order a sandwich. The person pointed up at a mouth-watering picture of a sandwich displayed on a hoarding above the counter and requested it.

The person standing behind the counter paused and looked at him. She said, "That's only for display. We don't make that one"

How unreasonable is it for a customer to expect that a sandwich that is prominently displayed and named and priced on the signage should actually be available to purchase? This is how life works under normal circumstances. In this instance, the sign offers something that the employees are unable or unwilling to provide. Luring people in with fancy sign or with offers that can't be fulfilled is just bad business. If you can't honor what you offer then you'll end up with the wrong kind of reputation.

3. Allow employees to disrespect your customers

> I was waiting in line recently for a coffee in a nearby shopping centre. They had one of those magnificent coffee making machines, gleaming ruby red and chrome. Behind the machine there were two ladies, working like fury to get the coffee made as efficiently as possible. The machine was slow though, so it was taking a little time to get the queue cleared. I was next in line, waiting for the person in front to collect their coffee so I could order mine.
>
> Just then an employee of the store edged up along the outside of the queue, glancing nervously at the line of people waiting to order. She leaned across in front of me towards the ladies behind the machine and said "Could you make me a cappuccino? I know you're busy". So what did the ladies behind the counter do? Well predictably enough they finished the order they were preparing, handed the coffees to the waiting customers, and then proceeded to prepare a cappuccino for this member of staff.

Does this drive customers crazy? Of course it does. When customers wait in line for service they expect to be served when it is their turn. How does being an employee entitle you to waltz past all the paying customers waiting in line? If you want to send a message to customers that you value them and their business then you need to show it. It's not enough to do it most of the time. You need to do it all of the time. Customers don't want to vie for seats and space with your employees. So for goodness sake, keep employees on their breaks away from customers and certainly don't encourage your employees to take liberties with customers. It's a really bad idea and demonstrates an utter lack of respect.

4. Stereotype your customers

It's curious how so many people working in customer-facing roles think they know all about their customer. They've seen it all before, and can spot "types" from a mile away. Or so they think. One of the absolute worst things you can do to your customer is to stereotype them. Yet it happens all the time. You look for a target audience, see if there are any obvious segments, and then define what will be sold to each and at what price. So why do we bother with stereotyping? A sales person might tell you that it allows them to make better use of their time, to be more efficient and effective. They may say that they can spot those who will buy and those who are just browsing. That's a typical justification. In truth there's not much to support this theory. In actual fact a customer's propensity to transact business depends on a number of factors, not least of which is the behaviour of the sales person.

Stereotypes are dangerous. They cause us to link things together in the mind that are not connected and are certainly not relevant. It's a lazy strategy that helps salespeople avoid doing what they should be doing. They need to work the room just like everyone else. Can you imagine someone working in a fruit and vegetable store segmenting their customers as they approach the fruit stalls? We connect high value products with the appearance or behaviour of the customer and we make value judgments and that's just a bad idea. If you want someone to buy from you then you must understand that your behaviour plays a pivotal role. Businesses need to realize that it's not good enough for members of staff to pick and choose which customers they will converse with. Businesses can't afford to make value judgments about potential customers based on how they look or behave when they walk through the door. When customers feel that salespeople are judging them it drives them crazy, it drives them away and straight to the door of a competitor who will behave as an adult and will treat them with the respect they deserve.

5. Completely ignore culture

The desire to homogenize customer service is a worldwide trend. However, the recognition of different cultural norms means that customer service standards will vary. Cultural expectations are not so easy to define. When we talk of culture we could mean national culture, corporate culture, or even regional culture. Culture, at its essence, relates to what people are used to where they come from. People are generally good at adapting to other cultures and when in a new place, they adopt many of the habits of people where they are. So, when you're responsible for providing a customer service experience you need to give some thought to the cultural dimension.

First and foremost you have to have an understanding of what is important to customers where you are. The easiest way to find this out is to ask them. Ask them what they value, what makes them choose your store or your product over others and what makes them come back again and again.

Second you need to be careful about who you put in front of the customer to deliver whatever it is that customers tell you they value. If for example they value the warmth and friendliness of your staff then those are the qualities to look for in the employees you put in the front office. This selection is driven by what you know about your individual members of staff and about the culture they were brought up in.

Each of us has our own individual interests, unique set of values and beliefs and possesses our own personal or family culture. It is reasonable to assume that people from a particular place in the world tend to understand that place and its practices and customs better than someone who was not brought up there. So when charged with creating an excellent customer service experience culture plays a role for sure. You need to understand something of what customers value and you need to put someone in front of the customer who understands that and who can deliver it effortlessly, consistently and most importantly with a genuine interest. Don't put a fake in front of customers.

6. Display a complete lack of understanding of what it means to be a customer

Is it frustrating is it to be a customer of your business? To what extent do your employees know this? Often employees know very little about what the customer experience is really like. This is especially true if your business sells a complex product or service. Most employees have been inducted into the business through some kind of on boarding programme for new employees. They learn about the business history, its values, the various products and services and so on. To fully train a new employee it is vital to provide a realistic perspective on what it means to be a customer. Your employee should know what happens when a customer tries to do business with you. An employee dealing with a call from an irate customer who wasted a day sitting at home waiting for an engineer who failed to show up will likely switch into the 'here's another moaning customer' mindset. They will likely utter some standard platitudes to try and appease the customer and may try to convince the customer to accept a rescheduled visit. If that employee has never experienced the utter frustration of the customer can they ever really empathize in a way that is genuine and authentic to the customer?

There's a lot to be gained from a walk in the customer's shoes to see what the customer experience is really like. Encourage staff at all levels of your business to go down to where a problem is and experience it first-hand. If you step into the customer's shoes and walk through the customer experience then you can witness first-hand how good or bad the experience really is.

Looking for the little issues

Another way to help your employees connect with this idea is to ask them all to make brief notes of the next time they are a customer of a similar business. Ask your staff to jot down the high and low points on the experience and to spot the little issues where the customer service experience is made great or is destroyed.

The idea is simple. You need your employees to "get" what it means to be a disgruntled customer. You need them to understand why customers sometimes get frustrated, annoyed and unreasonable. You need them to start developing a sense of where the problems start and what little things can be done to address tiny problems before they escalate into something much more serious. If you do this with your staff you are teaching them to fish in the customer service ocean. Don't waste all your time and money running expensive training programmes. Start by following the lesson of the Greek philosopher Socrates. Let them lead themselves to the logical conclusion through helping them ask the right questions. Once they have figured out what drives customers crazy it's time to run the formal training classes to add the finishing touches and to share the individuals' learning with everyone else.

☐

Key things to remember

- It's not enough to know how to use the tools you provide, employees need to know why.

- Help employees to deal with their own and their customers' emotions.

- Share what drives customers crazy so you can avoid it.

- Recognize the role and impact of culture on the service experience.

- Look out for the little issues before they get out of hand.

- Encourage employees to walk in the customers shoes and to understand what it feels like to be a customer.

PAUSE AND THINK

How certain are you that your employees understand what you are asking them to do, and why you are asking them to do it? Are you actively encouraging employees to engage in practices that drive customers crazy?

9 KEEP YOUR BEST PEOPLE CLOSE TO THE CUSTOMER

It has always struck me as a great paradox in modern business that individuals with the lowest paid jobs are among those with the greatest responsibility. Customer facing roles are a case in point. If your organisation is involved in selling something to customers or providing a service then it is clear who has the key responsibility of satisfying customers. Often businesses spend less and less time talking about customers and more and more time talking about stakeholders. The term stakeholder can mean anyone with a vested interest in the continued success of the business including your employees, your suppliers, your financiers, your partners and of course your customers.

You may also have people who own part or all of your business, usually in the form of shareholders. Sometimes, in the drive to satisfy shareholders, it is possible to overlook the other stakeholders mentioned above. In the drive to "maximize shareholder value" everything else becomes secondary. While most businesses tend to focus on reducing costs and maximizing profits in the short-term, history shows that investors enjoy significantly better returns from businesses that have a longer term orientation and a long term plan. Focusing only on delivering strong short-term financial results can have adverse effects on the long-term viability and attractiveness of your business. If you are planning to stay in business you need to take a long view of all stakeholder interests.

One of the biggest challenges in the modern customer service environment, whether we're talking about sales, support or any other customer facing activity, is keeping good people in the role for a viable amount of time. Good people don't stay long enough in customer facing roles because they see them as low-importance roles with limited career prospects. This has a particular impact on customers. Customers prefer to deal with the same person with whom they had a prior and positive customer service experience. When employees don't stay long in a job it means that when customers look for service it can feel like the service is random and impersonal. In many businesses today, it has become unrealistic for customers to expect to develop some kind of relationship with a specific person who can provide the service each time the customer needs it. Employees in customer facing roles feel a certain pressure to move on from these roles. They feel they need to move on to a "real job". Why is this?

The ramifications of focusing on status

One reason is purely financial. Customer service roles tend to be poorly paid compared with other roles. Another reason is psychological. It's connected to prestige. Customer service roles tend to be perceived and marketed as entry-level jobs.

These tend to be the roles that people start in when they join a business, progressing with time into more 'meaningful jobs'. Yet it's clear that the job of acting as the face of the business, being the representative of the business, is an important job if not the most important job. Customers see the person they are dealing with as the embodiment of the business. So why do we continue to treat these vital roles with something close to contempt? Why do we put new people in these roles and let them loose on customers? Why do we fail these roles? Why do we create the impression that all good people eventually get moved out of customer service? Earlier in this book I mentioned that it costs more money to attract a new customer than it does to retain an existing one and yet, who is charged with the responsibility of retaining the most important customers? The people in customer facing roles have an important responsibility. So why is it that many businesses pay these people comparatively low salaries and offer little or no incentive for people to stay in the role?

Anchoring the ones who fit

Some people just seem to be more naturally suited to roles that involve delivering a wonderful customer service experience. If this is true, and I really believe it is, then surely these employees belong right there, right in the situation where they come into contact with customers each and every day. They have the talent and the personality to make customers feel special; to make customers remain loyal and to turn yesterday's non-customers into today's new customers. They really are special and highly prized employees. You need and should want to keep these people in the place where they do their very best work. So why is it that these natural fit employees don't stay in the role? Well we've already answered that question. The role is perceived as a dead-end place to be. And it often doesn't pay very well.

Maybe it is time for you to have a conversation about this expectation to progress with each of your very best customer service professionals. Maybe it is time to explain clearly why you think their job is so important to your business and that they can and should expect a full and rewarding career in customer service. If you don't bother to tell them that customer service matters and is a real career option then you don't be surprised when you find out they think they need to leave to find a job with real career prospects. Don't assume they know that customer service really matters in your business. In many others it doesn't matter.

Customer service experts are not martyrs

You can't expect people to keep going the extra mile when it comes to providing service and support to your customers when you pay them poorly or fail to recognize their contribution. Equally you need to balance the importance of a role like customer service with the importance of other roles such as sales, management and so on. So what can you do? Well for a start you can show that you really do value the critical importance and critical contribution of your customer service people. I'm not talking about mentioning them in an e-mail to all staff. I'm not talking about paying lip service to them at your annual recognition event. I'm talking about something much more meaningful than that.

It's lazy and disingenuous to assume that your best customer service people might want to become managers. Typically people who are really good at something know they are really good at it, usually because everyone tells them so. They instinctively know that they have a talent for their special area and enjoy working at it. To these 'naturals' it doesn't even feel like work because they enjoy doing it so much. They don't want to walk away from it to do something else that pays better but feels uncomfortable. Yet that's exactly what so many people in this situation do. The way business works today, customer service professionals often feel that in order to get ahead they have to get out of doing what they do best.

This is counter-intuitive and counter-productive yet it happens all the time. People who are great at giving excellent customer service should be encouraged in every way possible to keep doing that. So what do you need to do? Well first off you need to recognize and celebrate each of your critical functions differently. This means that if you have sales people, you recognize and celebrated their success in a way that a sales person might appreciate, perhaps with some public praise or a bonus. If you have successful managers you might choose to recognize and celebrate their success at a lunch just for managers. Equally, you need to find the right way to recognize and celebrate your very best customer service employees with some form of customer service event. To create a special customer service event you could invite customers to come and describe why they remain loyal and satisfied customers or explain why the high quality service they receive really matters and what would happen to them if the service level dropped. Sales people might not be motivated by this information, nor might managers outside the customer service area.

When it comes to looking after customers like nobody else can, only people who devote themselves to excellence in customer service become energized by hearing their own customers say in their own words why they really value what customer service professionals do. Celebrate the excellence of your customer service people separately from other celebrations.

Of course we can easily measure sales results. When it comes to customer service, we may be able to measure if customers are satisfied but we can't easily show if this has a tangible effect on increasing sales or reducing costs. Sales results give us information about what is changing in the short-term. We know if we are selling more in a given period. When we measure customer service outputs we don't have any real indication of what the short-term business benefits might be. The outputs are not tangible enough for us to feel strongly about them. Yet we know that keeping the customer happy keeps the customer loyal, and we also know that keeping the customer loyal means making the next sale is easier and at a lower cost to the business. The reality is that most businesses today celebrate the performance of their sales people much more than they do their customer service people. There is a bias that favors sales and makes it seem that employees working in sales are somehow contributing something much more important than those in customer service. Both need to do an excellent job, yet the efforts of customer service employees are often overlooked. As a smart manager, you need to recognize the efforts and outputs of both, even when faced with a limited budget to do so. You can't continue to ignore your customer service employees while recognizing your sales people. You need to find relevant and genuine ways to recognize the efforts of your critically-important customer service employees so they know that you value what they do.

What about recognition?

As the old adage goes, money talks. If someone told you that you would spend all day dealing with customers who are angry, frustrated, disappointed or confused and that yours would be among the lowest paid jobs in the firm, would you take the job? Maybe you would if you were desperate for a job and willing to take any job. And that's exactly what you get when you pay low salaries for jobs like these. You get the wrong people taking the job for the wrong reasons. And we come back full circle to a group of disgruntled employees who hate their customers and hate their employer. You may not be able to offer high salaries but you may be able to offer a competitive base salary and some good benefits. A number of recent studies show that employees often value benefits as highly, or higher than, salary. Think carefully about what you could offer, and of course go and talk with your employees and find out what matters to them. Salary is important, but it's not the only thing employees care about.

Pay fairly for the nature of the work. And when you're saving money from reduced turnover costs, for heaven's sake channel some of those savings back into the pockets of those outstanding customer service employees who stay with you. You need them. Your business needs them. And most importantly your customers need them. Customer service people, those with the right predisposition, want to work with customers. They like solving problems. They like winning people over. Leave them alone to get on with it as they see fit and don't force them to leave because you don't or can't see the value of what they do.

Leave your best people alone

Find out who your best customer service employees are, pay them well, give them lots of incentives and recognition and leave them alone. Don't even think of promoting them if you risk losing their best value. As a business owner or manager you have to work hard to find ways to make them want to stay in the role.

In years gone by top-performing employees (using a very broad range of measures and perspectives) were nominated to attend conventions with their families, were given awards and vacations and so forth. The idea of rewarding the employee's performance with something the whole family could share made a lot of sense, especially when family time is often sacrificed to deliver the highest levels of commitment and performance. It was a way of paying something back to the family in return for their understanding. Nowadays we seem to view the employee as discrete and separate from their family once they enter the business premises. This is nonsensical and doesn't mirror the reality of how the personal lives and circumstances of employees are intertwined with their working day whether we like it or not.

Businesses often use individual career development and promotions to reward and recognize top performers. Rapid and unsustainable promotion and advancement has resulted in employees spending more time away from families, even greater personal sacrifice and has created an unsustainable trend of promotion-chasing that businesses and whole industries cannot afford. Clearly not everyone can be the boss, yet top performers have all been set on a path to the top that can only end in disappointment for most: not everyone can be promoted. So when businesses put the emphasis on promotion and then dream up ways to create "pseudo promotions" by changing job titles, seniority, salaries, terms and conditions of employment and by offering stock options or a company vehicle, they need to think about how likely this incentive is to make a positive impression on the employee's whole life and not just their individual work life.

In practice, the person who comes to work every day for you brings all the baggage of family, lifestyle, personal interests and everything else. The employee does not stop being interested in, or impacted by, all those elements that make up their personal life once they enter their place of work. Smart businesses look for ways to extend the attractiveness of the role to the individual. Broadening the range of incentives to include things that you know the person will enjoy keeps a role rewarding and engaging for the individual. When thinking about reward and recognition stop thinking that promotions, role changes and extra responsibility are what everyone wants. It's simply not true. Instead consider adopting a personalized approach to employee rewards and recognition. Give serious and genuine consideration to rewards that demonstrate that you have really thought about the reward. For example instead of an unimaginative and generic reward consider offering specially chosen tickets to sporting events, concerts, family meals at a restaurant, family fun days, and so on. By demonstrating personalization in your approach to reward and recognition you are signaling that you have noticed more than just an employee's performance. You have noticed your employee's interests and acted on the information and this exhibits great management on your part.

Now more than ever there is a need to keep great people firmly rooted in roles that take advantage of their unique talents. You need them to stay but more importantly you need them to be content and settled in the role. You need them to put down roots for the years ahead. As long as the employee knows that you're working hard to find ever more ways to keep them there doing what they do best they'll keep coming in to work and doing a great job.

The dangers of generalizing

Resist the temptation to aggregate the needs of your employees to earn economies of scale. This is a well-intentioned but ultimately disastrous idea. People are not the same and most definitely don't want the same thing. So resist the urge to believe the motivations and desires of all people to be the same. Resist the urge to stereotype. Resist the urge to conclude that all employees will have the same motivation from work. They simply don't. Design something that will be attractive to each valued employee and will send a message to individuals that the business is looking, listening and learning.

The measurement paradox

Every business needs a way to know how it is doing. Any business worth its salt will have a set of measurable targets that it focuses on as it tries to achieve its strategic objectives. It also needs a mechanism to allow it to monitor those targets and correct for performance deficiencies. Some years ago this idea came to prominence with the introduction of *The Balanced Scorecard*[16]. Kaplan and Norton's Balanced Scorecard suggested that there was more to business success than focusing on revenue, costs and profit. Kaplan and Norton suggested that in order to be successful over time, a firm must pay attention to a number of areas of the business, such as financial performance, customer performance, internal business processes and organizational learning and growth. While the idea caught on very quickly, not every business was able to generate a mechanism to allow the business performance in key strategic areas to be easily checked. Not only can it be difficult to set up ways to monitor performance, those businesses that did find a way to monitor target performance often fell into the trap of measuring the wrong thing. Sadly this is still a serious problem in modern organisations when it comes to tracking business performance.

All too often organisations claim that a certain value or standard is central to their business while at the same time employees are rewarded for doing something entirely different. In the worst cases employees may even be rewarded for doing the exact opposite of what the organisation claims in public to be its most important focus. In his book The Toyota Way[17], author Jeffrey Liker notes that Toyota attributes much of its success in the area of leadership succession to a special focus on removing business metrics that create behaviour which conflicts with the ideals and norms of the organisation. For example you can't claim that respect for the environment is a key strategic driver of your business when behind the scenes managers are choosing courses of action that have dire environmental consequences because they are rewarded for something else entirely, such as driving down costs. If you ask employees to deliver A but reward them for B then it should be no surprise that they will focus on delivering B. If you want excellent customer service but routinely reward employees by moving them out of customer service then you are contradicting your supposed commitment to customer service. Likewise if you ask employees to move mountains to make sure customer satisfaction is excellent yet punish employees who incur costs in order to fix problems then you surely can't be surprised when employees stop going the extra mile. After all you've set a powerful punishment precedent.

When you promote your employee are you demoting your customer?

Author Peter Senge[18] presented the concept of Systems Thinking as an approach that can be adopted at times of critical decision-making. It allows those making the decision to anticipate and understand the consequences of a decision as it ripples through an entire organisation or system. Developing this capability allows leaders and managers to see the far-reaching consequences of what seems like a local decision. When considering changing the face of the business, all aspects and potential effects need to be considered. Overcoming challenging situations from the past can give a false sense of security, leading us to thinking we are brilliant at adapting and flexing to accommodate change. Previous experience of saying "we'll work it out somehow" and a few solid examples of managing to somehow pull it off at the last moment make us feel pretty resilient and pretty confident about our ability to solve problems that life may throw at us.

    Short-term decision making that focuses on fixing the immediate problem will almost always come back and hurt you. This is especially true when it concerns moving someone who is doing a great job into a new position. You really can't make a decision like this on a whim or a gut feeling. It's not about the simple decision of whether to move the person or not. It's about all the consequent decisions it then presents. Who will replace this person and who will replace that person in turn? And on it goes. By making your decision based only on one tiny piece of the picture you run the risk of blindsiding yourself to potentially bigger and more far-reaching problems. Take the time you need to get all the information you can before you even think about moving great people around inside your organisation.

Promotion is not always the best option

Virtually every professional business will feature at least one well known example of the Peter Principle , named after Laurence J. Peter, a Canadian academic. Peter's simple and compelling insight that in a hierarchy an employee will tend to rise to their "level of incompetence" encapsulates the problem that most businesses face, especially those that serve customers directly. It means that organisations tend to promote people into roles for which they are utterly unsuitable. Here's an example of how it often happens.

Susan works in a retail store, serving customers. The customers love her and constantly rave about her to her manager. The business desperately wants to retain her so they promote her, and make her a supervisor. The new job means a lot more responsibility but Susan still gets to spend a good deal of time dealing with customers. Susan does a good job so the business still wants to keep her.

They promote her to manager. Susan is not sure if this is the right move for her but thinks the career aspect of the move is too good to turn down. Susan gets an office at the back of the store, a stack of weekly reports and data sheets and has to quickly learn the skills of being a people manager and a store manager. She works hard but it's not as enjoyable as either of her old jobs. She eventually starts to master the skills required and soon starts to get on top of things. The business notices and decides that they want to promote her to area manager.

Susan will get a pay-rise, a business car and will have a group of store managers reporting to her. She'll need to get up earlier in the morning to make sure that she'll have time to travel the great distances between stores, and should expect to get home a little later in the evening. But it's worth it, or so she is told by the business. Susan tries it for a little while, hates it and quits.

What's so wrong with that I hear you ask? Well, not much on the face of it. Opportunities came along and Susan worked hard to earn them. In the end she just couldn't handle the pressure. Right? Not necessarily. The Peter Principle[19] teaches us that sometimes we pluck people out of jobs at which they are outstanding. We think, mistakenly, that maybe if people apply the same ethic in a more senior position then the business will reap the benefits. Sometimes this is true. Sometimes it is not.

Writer and researcher Marcus Buckingham suggests in his book Now Discover Your Strengths[20] that we each are programmed genetically to excel at certain things while at the same time we each have things at which we'll never really be any good. Yet the modern mantra is that people can be molded, shaped and trained to do almost anything. As humans we have always instinctively known that we do our best work in areas in which we have a deep interest and some obvious talent. It makes no sense to take your best customer service professionals and move them into roles that take away their opportunity to do excellent work every day. So the counter argument is offered: If I can't move them into new roles then what do I do to retain them in my business?

Ask yourself if it is possible to keep the person in the role, keep them doing what they excel at, yet somehow find ways to keep them interested in staying in the role indefinitely.

If you are serious about customer service and about keeping your best customer service professionals in roles where they can have a real and lasting positive impact on your customers then you should consider formally identifying your best customer service professionals as your customer service heroes. Send them out into the world to represent you. Assign them to help out new people who join your organisation. Certainly pay them more and offer them the same perks and benefits that you offer to top performers in other parts of your business. Give them the use of a company vehicle. Give them family vacation tickets. Do anything that shows that what they do is enormously valuable. Just don't promote them out of a great fitting job.

The impossibility of getting everyone onboard

If you are interested in customer service you will almost certainly have come across the legend of the Wal-Mart song. In his book Made in America[21] Wal-Mart founder Sam Walton explains how it was customary for staff at Wal-Mart stores to gather before store opening and sing the company song. Wal-Mart had a company song because the founder and president Sam Walton thought it was a good way of rallying people around a common cause, his vision of what Wal-Mart was all about. Whether it actually engendered loyalty, or increased performance or productivity depends on each employee's viewpoint. If the employee tended to be already committed to Wal-Mart and really wanted to work there and do a great job, then the song definitely did. If you were a reluctant employee with a casual approach to your work and with no real long-term interest in working at Wal-mart or serving customers, then you probably might have thought it was the dumbest thing you had ever heard.

Another business you can't fail to come across when looking at customer service legends is Nordstrom. Nordstrom has a unique culture among employees. They stick together, learn together, serve customers together and compete together. They really want to do an outstanding job.
Is this approach to bonding employees together likely to appeal to every employee? In his book Built to Last[22] author Jim Collins answers this question definitively. Dictating that every employee must fully embrace a single way of working and behaving will not work. Examine these overarching policies in action at a typical fast food restaurant or supermarket. Does everyone smile? Does everyone look happy to see you in the store? The challenge with rallying around a song or group training is that they only improve the performance of people who really believe in what the business is trying to do, and who connect with the vision of the future. These people feel engaged and want to be part of that future. This requires them to take actions every day to move another step towards that future. If, on the other hand, they don't give a damn about the business's future then they really won't show much effort to move the business toward the future. Disengaged employees might fake it for a while but sooner or later they will be gone. They will quit or they will get fired.

How well are we really doing?

Most businesses want to know what customers think about their products and services, the quality of customer service they provide, their customers' likelihood to buy again and so on. Large businesses, in particular, pay good money to gather this information. Sadly most approach this task in a way that wastes time, money, and a valuable opportunity to have direct contact with a customer. Businesses Typically engage an external firm to design a survey and roll it out to customers. These days this involves sending a link in an email or SMS message to an online survey, placing a survey on a prominent website, or by a swathe of calls from a call centre asking customers if they would be willing to spend a few minutes answering mindless questions using Likert-scale type responses that defy reasoning over the phone.

In a number of contributions to the Harvard Business Review, Frederick Reichheld[23] suggests that such approaches to learning about customer service are a waste of time. In his view these approaches represent a massive waste of effort and disrespect the time of your valuable customers. He also suggests that often the wrong people respond, skewing the so-called 'market intelligence' that these surveys are designed to provide. In his view, the only way to get this information is to get out and talk to your customers. But who could you possibly trust to get out and talk to your customers?

If you already have brilliant, highly regarded, trustworthy people working in your organisation who consistently deliver outstanding customer service and love what they do, then get them out in front of your customers. This is a wonderful way to keep these gems motivated and engaged. Send them to listen to your customers and let them find out what really is good and bad. Let them hear it first hand from real customers. They'll bring the message back unfiltered and unedited because they care and they will want to remain involved in solving the problems that they encountered. They might even want to personally call people back. Get them out there, give them a stack of personalized business cards and let your best people connect directly with your best customers.

Why would you want an anonymous person working for a third-party market research organisation asking your customer questions when you've already got the best qualified person inside your organisation already?

☐

Key things to remember

- Look carefully at the messages you are sending about how you value customer service.

- What incentive is there for people to want to work in customer service or move there from another department?

- Differentiate between anchoring and being stuck in a rut.

- Reward people for the valuable work they do.

- Stop unsettling your best people with daft promotion paths that damage your business and their careers.

- Don't ever assume that you know what people want, there is no such thing as 'people' when it comes to motivation - it's an individual thing.

- Make sure you are measuring the right things.

- Use your best people to listen to your customers - don't outsource your conversations to third parties.

PAUSE AND THINK

What does promotion mean inside your organisation? Do people have to turn their backs on what they are good at in order to get ahead? Do people really believe that customer service is important? Is that reflected in status and reward? How well do you really know your employees and what they want?

10 MAPPING THE CUSTOMER SERVICE SYSTEM

If you are serious about making customer service a critical part or *the* critical part of your business strategy then you need to prepare yourself for a transformation. Most businesses have made the mistake of hiring people who don't belong there and who don't care enough about what the business is trying to do. Transformation means: having the right people on-board; making sure everyone is clear about what they are required to do and how to do it; making sure everyone knows why they are doing it; and finally moving from talking about doing it to actually doing it. There should be no surprises. To make that a reality, you need to think about the steps required and the sequence in which they should happen.

The term "transformation" implies moving from one place or state to another. In order to do that effectively it is important to not only know where you want to get to but equally where you are now. You must have a full appreciation for where you are right now in terms of your customer service performance before you even think about transforming to a higher level of performance.

Beware of bias

As human beings we all suffer from bias. Bias occurs when we are confident that we have experienced something before and therefore make a broad assumption about it in order to save time and get more quickly to a decision. This can be dangerous in business. It leads to the stereotyping discussed earlier, it leads to assumptions about what customers and employees want, and it leads to disastrous decisions that could ruin your business. Bias is a demonstration of laziness, of a lack of effort to really scrutinize what lies in front of us. Efforts to understand the business and where you are now will never be entirely free of bias because we all have prior experience that colors our view of what we see.

It is common to consider using external partners to carry out an assessment of where the business stands today. Often these external partners will play the bias card and will claim to have a more objective, dispassionate perspective on your business and situation that you do. This is rarely true in practice. While you will get access to often excellent researchers and solid methods of research, it will come at a high price. For small businesses this is simply not a viable option.

For small businesses I would suggest that to get the best result from this kind of research it makes more sense to use your own staff, avoiding the big costs associated with hiring an outside research firm. The other huge advantage you have when considering doing this important work yourself is that your own people know your customers, know the products and services you are offering, and *want* to deeply understand your customers. Using your own people to mine this rich source of information allows you to build internal capability and maximize the knowledge gathering phase while carefully managing your own biases and prior experiences with customers.

Where to begin?

There is really only one place to begin. Begin with your customers. You need to know what your customers experience when they interact with your business. You need to know what they buy and why, remembering that they may not actually really know why they buy from you. You might even find out why they *don't* buy from you. You need to know everything you can possibly find out. You especially need to know what their expectations are when it comes to customer service. Do they expect to be able to call you every hour of the day, on every day of the week? Do they expect people on the phone at your organisation to know everything immediately? Do they expect someone will call them back within a certain time period? You really need this information. You also need to take a walk in your customers' shoes. Step into their experience of what it really is like to do business with your own people. This can be incredibly revealing. And while all this is going on, find out what customers think about why you are in business, what the business is trying to do for customers, why it exists and so on. The answers will likely be very revealing about your organization's marketing effort, your brand and how it is viewed out there in the real world. You will find out how good you really are.

What next?

Gathering information about what customers expect and demand from your organisation will be highly valuable but by no means is it all that you will need to know. You also need to carefully consider what customers tell you they are willing to spend money on, what products and services they actually value and why. This should inform your decision making as you think about how you will concentrate your efforts going forward. Customer service is all about knowing and meeting expectations. When you are armed with information from the customers' own mouths about their expectations you can align your organization's resources to better meet those expectations. By thinking about the expectations you intend to meet you will be able to build a clear picture of what kind of organisational structures will be needed to fulfill those customer service requirements. At this point you are about to map your customer service system.

A system, not a chain

I mentioned previously Michael Porter's concept of the value chain[24], a way of viewing all of the interdependent and interconnected elements of an organisation that must work together cohesively to deliver the overall strategic objectives and business results. In Porter's model the activities inside an organisation that directly contribute to producing something (a product or service) for a customer are referred to as primary activities, while those that are largely unseen by customers are referred to as secondary or support activities. The model that value is derived when there are effective linkages inside the organisation.

While the value chain provides a useful model for showing how the elements must link together it does not show the critical interdependencies that exist between *all* the elements. To show this we must take a *system* view of the inside of an organisation. The system view implies that each separate element inside the organisation depends on the other parts in order to function correctly. Think of the organisation as being like a finely balanced ecosystem such as a forest; willful neglect of one part of the ecosystem could have a devastating effect on the balance of the entire ecosystem causing eventual failure. Equally, changing something in one part of the system can often produce unintended consequences in another part of the system, hence the need to view the entire system when dealing with the big decisions that face an organisation. The system view of the organisation is a more appropriate way to view the organisation when it comes to customer service. No amount of effort to create satisfied and loyal customers will mean anything if one part of the organisation is systemically destroying the customer experience.

Mapping the customer service system

To understand the connections between your organisation and your customers you need a map of your *customer service system, or CSS*. This will show all the parts and how they need to fit together in a coherent fashion to deliver the desired level of customer service and your desired business outcomes. Your *customer service system* should show all areas of your organisation that play a part, directly or indirectly, in producing something that creates value for your customer. Once you have mapped your CSS, you can then start assessing the quality of relationships between the different parts of the system, the flow of critical information between the parts, and whether each part has the resources it needs. Vitally, you can also determine if each part in the system is clear about its objectives, and if it is clear about how it should operate so that employees are guided to do the right thing in the right way.

By defining and mapping your entire customer service system you can identify all the various component parts that play a role in shaping how customer service is delivered and supported by your entire organisation. This will provide you with two immediate benefits. First, you can establish how each individual part is performing. Second, you can assess the quality of the linkages between parts, what we normally refer to as relationships. You can work out which groups enjoy positive relationships when working together, and which groups are experiencing difficult relationships or have experienced a complete breakdown.

The detailed mapping of your entire customer service system allows you to assess the impact of things like HR policies, management practices, and the strategic decisions on the performance of the customer service system. This links critical management decisions to the impact they have on those who deal directly with your customers every day.

An organisation that wants to tap into the full value of customer service will take time to understand the full customer service system that exists today inside the business. So, how does a business go about developing this understanding? The next few sections will show how you can go about mapping your customer service system and in doing so, develop an understanding of what customer service is like today and what you need to do to take it to another level.

Who should have contact with your customers?

You don't want your customers to be exposed to all the issues and internal challenges facing your organisation. While honesty is almost always the best policy, sometimes too much information provided to your customer can introduce unnecessary anxiety and scare your customers away. If you have problems with product shipments or delayed deliveries then that's really an internal issue and should not be shared automatically with your customers. If you have problems with a driver who didn't make it in to work today you need to deal with that internally. And how many times does one of your own technical experts frighten a customer away by listing all the competitive shortcomings of your product when in truth the product does everything the customer really values?

You need to control the interface with your customer because sometimes your organisation can be its own worst enemy. You need to decide which people are best placed to help the customer directly and which people are better served doing their work behind the scenes and far away from the customer.

Placing the customer at the centre of the system

When envisioning a customer service system think of the customer as the centre of the world, as shown below. The customer service people and the sales people from the organisation should be placed closest to the customer. These are the only people who should have regular direct contact with your customer.

In practice, a relationship with a customer usually has its origins in a potential customer making some form of contact with your organisation, often to explore a potential sale or transaction. Ideally this 'pre-sale'

conversation should take place between the potential customer and your customer service people. If the dialogue is satisfactory to the customer and products or services from your business can clearly meet their needs, the customer can be expected to proceed and engage with your sales people. This is a critical stage since this is often where commitments are made and expectations are set. The sales people and customer service people in your organisation must share a common understanding of the capabilities of your business, of what can realistically be delivered by your business and therefore what expectations can be set *and* met for a customer.

If the customer has any post-sale queries, problems or concerns the dialogue can be easily restarted with your customer service people and outstanding requirements can be attended to. This again is a vital stage, since the overarching purpose of the process is to build customer loyalty and satisfaction, with the clear purpose of retaining the customer so that they return and conduct further business with your organisation..

By delivering an excellent pre-sale customer experience, properly setting and meeting expectations and honestly communicating capabilities during the sale, and comprehensively addressing any post sale customer requirements you can create a *virtuous triangle* of sustainable customer loyalty and repeat business with your customer.

When customers need more

Because each business is different, the reasons for providing customer service will vary from firm to firm. Therefore, you need to think carefully about your entire organisation, and with whom your customer should have direct contact. Only you can decide what is best for your organisation, however the following diagram indicates how an appropriate customer service system might be structured in a modern organisation.

A Customer Service System (CSS)

The diagram suggests that not all the elements of your customer service system need to be directly accessed by your customer. Your customer should always have direct access to your sales people and your customer service people. Ideally, there should be a wall separating the customer from all of the 'behind the scenes' operations of your business. If a customer encounters a problem with your business, they may need access behind this first wall, such as to someone in technical support or someone in marketing. In practice, any connection by a customer to a part of your business behind this wall should be handled and managed by your customer service people.

Further back in the system, behind a second wall, are typically functions that provide organisational support to the customer service system, but to which your customer would not normally require access. There are very few scenarios where a customer, under normal circumstances, would require direct access to your IT department or a member of your management team, for example.

The overall aim of establishing a *customer service system* is to deliver a consistent and appropriate level of customer service according to the expectations of customers without exposing the customer to the complexity 'behind the scenes' of your organisation. A properly mapped *customer service system* shows what groups have a direct and indirect impact on your organization's capacity to deliver a high level of service. Looking at the previous diagram, you can see instantly that things that happen in one part of the system, in manufacturing & production for example, can lead to a direct impact on the customer care or support staff. Equally changes in ICT (information and communications technology) such as a new phone system or new customer relationship database can dramatically impact the level of service experienced by customers.

Establishing what all the parts are that make up your customer service system is the first stage of what is required. Once you can see the system laid out in all its parts you can start to think about questions such as:

- How many people do we have in Sales?
- How many people do we have in Customer Service?
- How do the people in Customer Service get information about new products before our customers do?
- What other parts of our business have direct contact with customers? Do they need this direct contact?

By completing a customer service system assessment you will also have a chance later to reflect carefully on the impact of thinks such as business strategy, leadership style, HR policies and management practices on customer service. You will be able to look at the system and assess if recent or planned changes are likely to impact the level of service provided, allowing you to identify options for remedying any likely problems at various points in the system.

Problems, people, and processes

Once you start looking at your customer service system you will begin to recognize areas that could threaten your capacity to deliver and sustain an outstanding customer service. However, you need to be careful not to rush to judgment when looking at things with new eyes. The customer service system is a complex system, with everything connected to everything else. Senge's 'Systems thinking'[25] teaches us that small changes at a single point in a system can have enormous consequences in another part of the system, often unseen. You need to be careful and considered when looking at your customer service system.

In order to make any decisions about what to do, you need a full and realistic appraisal of the complete system. While it's tempting to start with an immediate review of your people, often in the form of managers sitting around a table working their way down a list of employees and deciding who should stay and who should go, in practice this is not a smart way begin. It is not wise to automatically assume that people are the cause of your service issues. Often the usual people solutions (re-training or recruitment) will not address issues around customer service.

What should my Customer Service System look like?

Try following the shape of the customer service system (CSS) shown in Figure 3. Ideally when you are sketching out your CSS you should strictly limit the parts of the business that need daily and direct contact with your customer. In my view that means sales and customer service.

Those two groups, sales and customer service, will typically depend on other functions to supply them with information that they need in order to service the customer or sell something to the customer, so the question is which groups possess this information and can directly supply the information to customer service and sales? These groups should sit at the next or second level of your CSS.

Finally there will be groups that have an indirect bearing on your sales and customer service functions, providing high-level guidance and direction and policies. These groups, such as HR and Management, sit in the next layer again of your CSS.

You can set out your CSS in any way you like, as long as it makes clear the point that some groups need direct access to the customer, and some groups don't.

Is this my new organization chart?

The CSS is definitely not your new organization chart. The organization chart (or 'org chart' for short) shows how responsibility is divided up across the organisation. The organization chart shows who holds responsibility in each area of the business for delivering business results, such as sales revenue, profit, cost management, employee recruitment etc.

The CSS is something entirely different. It shows all of the people that have a responsibility for delivering an excellent customer service experience, and what share of that responsibility is held in each part of the business. The CSS shows which parts of the business have a direct influence on the customer experience, which areas have a secondary influence on the customer experience, and which areas have a background influence when it comes to customer service. In the next section we'll see how the CSS is used to assess how clear and focused your people are in each area of your business about what is required to deliver a great customer service experience.

One final point. Don't overcomplicate the effort involved in mapping your CSS. You can spend a lot of time laying it out in Microsoft Visio or Adobe Illustrator but I'm a big fan of using a flip chart and some sticky notes to try and work out what are all the parts and where do they all fit. Don't worry about it being perfect or precise. Just try and get a picture of what all the parts are and roughly where they should fit.

11 UNDERSTANDING YOUR REALITY

Once you have a picture of all the parts that make up your business and where you believe they fit in your Customer Service System, it's time to find out how you work today and where there might be gaps in the way your business works with customers. This will involve spending a little time meeting people around the business and asking them questions to understand what they know and think about how the business works. By asking questions and developing an understanding you will quickly figure out which important knowledge, skills and attitudes are missing as you try to improve the customer experience. More importantly, this next stage will involve you asking yourself and your management team (if you have one) how good a job you are doing in some absolutely crucial areas that affect customer service.

What questions do I need to ask? What am I trying to understand?

You could waste a lot of time striking up general conversations with employees or reflecting on your business by yourself or with your management team and never really learn what you need to learn. Without some clear guidance about what matters most there's a danger that you will waste time talking and thinking about things that really won't be valuable.

Instead, I suggest you focus on seven specific areas, what I call "the seven Ps of customer service". By exploring these seven areas you will develop a clear picture of where you really are today when it comes to customer service.

You may be thinking at this stage that you don't have time to spend thinking about or talking about these subjects. If you invest the time, and I'm deliberately using the word 'invest' here, you will learn a huge amount about your current state of your business and the current capabilities and attitudes of your employees. You'll also give yourself the chance to start in the right place. If you don't spend time on this your chances of making any real and lasting improvements will be close to zero. In practice you don't need to spend huge amounts of time thinking about this or meeting everyone in your business. Aim to set aside a few hours at the start to think about the answers to the important questions that need answering. Equally, you only need to speak to a reasonable sample of your employees should to get the insights you need, as long as the sample of employees is somewhat random. "Cherry picking" your most-positive or most-critical employees will severely skew the information that comes back.

Finally, when it comes to meeting with employees you don't have to ask the questions. You can pick someone competent and trustworthy to meet the employees and ask the questions, but you must brief them fully on what you want them to do and why you are doing it to make sure they understand the purpose of the exercise.

Exploring the organization to understand where you are

It's a good idea to explore the seven areas in sequence if at all possible. Avoid skipping areas too since each one is critically important to your customer service system. The seven areas that you should explore by yourself or with other employees, the seven Ps of customer service as I called them earlier, are:

1. Purpose
2. Product
3. Performance
4. People
5. Power
6. Procedures
7. Possibilities

Between them, they contain the key information you need in order to realistically and accurately assess the current state of customer service in your business.

Start by looking at the Purpose.

Before you even think about meeting with employees it makes sense for you to ask yourself some questions first about the **Purpose** of the business. It's always a good idea to start with 'the why' before looking at anything else. What you're trying to determine here is if the purpose of your organisation is really as clear and well understood as you believe it to be. Time and time again a perception gap exists in organisations between those at the top (who decide and explain the strategy) and those further down within the organisation (to whom the strategy message is communicated). It's a good idea to ask yourself some of these questions first. Then go and speak to a few employees in different parts of the business to find out if they see it like you do.

Checklist of questions about the Purpose of the company

- What steps have you taken to make the purpose of your business absolutely clear and simple to understand?
- How recently have you examined this purpose to check that it is still relevant and appropriate?
- What steps have you taken to communicate the purpose of your business with your employees?
- How exactly did you go about communicating the purpose?
- To whom did you direct the communication effort? Did you forget anyone?
- What type of communication did you use? (email, meeting, poster etc.)
- How long did the communication effort last? (1 message, a week of messages, continuous etc.)

What are your own responses to the questions above telling you about how clear the purpose of your business is? How well understood do you believe (or hope) it is across the business? Do you feel you have put enough effort into making sure that everyone knows what the business is trying to do? At this point it would be a good idea to strike up some conversations around the business to see what other people think the purpose of the business is.

Next it's important to look at your **Product** to find out which product(s) or services offered by your company are truly valued by customers, which products are damaging your reputation, and whether there is a 'reality gap' that exists inside the organisation.

Checklist of questions about your Product

- Where could I find a full list of all the offerings that make up the portfolio of products and services offered by your business?
- Who decides on what is added and what is removed from the

portfolio?
- How frequently are products/services added or removed from the portfolio of offerings? When did it last happen? What was added or removed?
- How do you check that staff and customers understand what is in the portfolio? Where do customers get their information?
- When was this last checked? Who checked the understanding of customers? Who checked that staff know the full list of what is sold?
- When was the last time a check was made on assumptions about what the customer wants and values from the business? Who checked this?
- Who is responsible for making sure that customer needs and expectations are fully understood? When was this last assessed?

While you may be able to answer these questions yourself, it will be vitally important for you to get the views of employees for a balanced perspective.

Performance is assessed next. It is the measure that proves to you that being in business makes sense. It's your way of knowing if your business delivers more output than input. Often the assessment of actual performance can be one of the most difficult things to do in business, since a large and varied set of daily activities inside a business can hide a whole host of problems and costs. Sometimes a long, hard look with an objective eye can suggest that many businesses are no longer worth sustaining. It's time to figure out how your business is doing if you don't already know.

Checklist of questions about your Performance

- How realistic is your measurement of performance?
- Are you capturing live (by the minute) data, daily, weekly or over longer intervals? Who is responsible for the quality of the data that is captured?
- Where is the data stored? Who has access to it? Can they see everything or only some of it?
- How frequently do you or your managers get updated information?
- Is the data actually used to make business decisions? Does it mean something or must it be 'translated' for it to become valuable?
- Is the data gathering and sharing fully automated? Does someone spend lots of time punching numbers into Excel in order to make

the data useable?
- Do employees and managers trust the data? Has it ever been wrong and caused a problem or incident?

The assessment of your **People** is so critical that if you fail to do this right you could be hastening your own slow and inevitable demise. You need to know if you have the right people on board, what skills they have, and how those skills are deployed every day (or not) and how they feel about working for you and with their customers. You need to know how your employees feel about how they are managed, how they are regarded and how they are communicated with. And you need to know if they are thinking of leaving for a better opportunity.

Checklist of questions about your People

- What measures or policies exist to ensure that there is a continuous supply of outstanding people joining the business?
- What is the process or policy for promotions and succession inside the business?
- Who decides which person will take over when someone leaves the business?
- How are people managed inside the business? Are people tightly controlled or allowed to find their own best way to do things?
- Is the approach to people management different across different departments? Does the approach vary greatly depending on the manager?
- How much guidance do managers get from the business about how they should work with their people?
- Do managers enjoy their jobs? Do they take their jobs seriously?
- Do employees aspire to be managers and why/why not? Is it a respected position?
- Are there examples of people in management roles who should not be?
- Are managers under more or less pressure than regular employees?
- Are management practices inside the business something that competitors or rivals would be likely to copy?

Research from various sources including the London School of Economics[26] suggests that managers are often very poor judges of their own performance. For this reason it is imperative that you seek as broad a range of inputs as possible. Asking employees for their comments on management can feel very dangerous, especially when employees are not often asked for their opinion and may be suspicious of what might happen to the data. You may need to increase the employees' sense of safety to comment about management by using a neutral person that they trust, possibly even someone from outside the company with whom they feel they can be honest. Don't underestimate the importance of psychological safety and the need to reassure employees that their feedback and comments will be handled with care and discretion.

Another important aspect of your Customer Service System is **Power**, specifically the degree to which people are encouraged and empowered to do their best work every day. It's important for you to know if they feel they have the power to do the right thing for customers and for the business, or if they feel trapped and burdened by red tape and unwieldy rules and controls.

Checklist of questions about Power

- How is employee work supervised? Who supervises it? How frequently is it supervised and how closely?
- Have employees been consulted recently about the level of supervision?
- Do employees get any feedback after supervision? Who gives the feedback and what do they say? What do employees feel about this feedback?
- Do employees receive coaching and what form does the coaching take? Who does the coaching? Is it helpful to the employee?
- What objectives and performance goals are written down for each employee? Who decides on these goals? Where do these goals come from?
- Are employees' goals linked to any other goals? Are the goals realistic and fair from the employee perspective?
- Are the employee goals fair and realistic from the manager's perspective?
- Are the goals orientated towards maintaining standards or raising standards? Are any rewards linked to these goals?
- Who carries out the review that determines the final review of the year's performance?
- Are goals modified or updated during the year?
- What happens if performance remains the same over a year? What

happens if performance deteriorates? How do you know if performance has changed?
- Is there a team or group performance target?
- Is there a limit to the number of employees that can be rated as top performers?
- Does anyone outside the team or group act as an independent reviewer of performance?

An assessment of **Procedures** is important but it must be carried out with the right focus. All too often an assessment like this often results in a range of new procedures and management systems being introduced to ensure that there is a process for everything. That's not what is being advocated here at all. Instead, the point of this assessment is to determine if your procedures are either harming customer service or making it better. This assessment will challenge the need for everything to be documented and will assess if procedures need to be created, improved, or removed altogether.

Checklist of questions about Procedures

- What mechanisms and systems exist to track if employees are following defined procedures?
- To what extent are all key procedures clearly and accurately documented?
- How often are staff consulted about the efficacy of procedures?
- How would you know if a procedure is actually getting in the way of customer service? When did this last happen?
- Are staff ever forced to go against the wishes of their customers?
- How would you detect that procedures are causing frustration and stress in employees? How would you test the same for customers?
- Have any employees ever left the business due to their dissatisfaction with the procedures they were required to follow? How could you find this out?
- How familiar are you with what other leading organisations do when it comes to procedures around customer service?
- Is it obvious to customers when employees are walking them through a set procedure?
- Do customers ever react negatively to being walked through a procedure? How are such reactions handled?

The final part of the assessment is **Possibilities**. You need to know if your employees sense the possibilities the future may hold, not in terms of promotions and compensation but in terms of job interest, personal growth, challenge and anything else that might serve to motivate each individual. Likewise your customers should share their perspective on future possibilities and can be a rich source of future business opportunity, but that can only happen if you include them in your assessment.

But it's not all about sensing the positives about the future. A huge determinant of a positive customer experience is a positive aspect in the employee dealing with the customer. If the employee holds a disaffected view on the business, or has lost faith in the future because of a loss of confidence in management, this can often show up in very subtle ways in the customer interaction. It is vital that you use this part of the assessment to gauge the mood and disposition around the company.

Checklist of questions about Possibilities

- Do employees ever discuss the future of the organisation? How do they envisage their own role in the organisation in the future?
- How do they portray the customer service encounter of the future?
- Would you characterize the employee description of the future as positive, negative or neutral?
- What do employees say when discussing their role, their prospects and their future opportunities in a typical employee-manager review meeting?
- What sense do you have of the place that work fills in the lives of employees?
- How hard does top management try to keep the most talented employees with the business?
- How much awareness does top management have of employee satisfaction levels in different parts of the business?
- How much awareness does top management have of what customers think of employees in these parts of the business?
- Do employees feel that top management understands what it means to do the employee's job?
- Do employees have confidence in their direct manager or in top management?
- What does top management do to improve the employee experience?

- What does top management do to tap even more into the skills and unseen capabilities of employees? Where is the proof of these efforts?
- Who is responsible for maximizing the contribution of individual employees?

Living Room, Helicopter and Engine Room

In order to carry out a comprehensive assessment you should consider looking at your company from a variety of perspectives. First, you might consider observing your business from the living rooms of the customers who buy your goods and services. They know what it is *really* like to transact business with you.

Equally you need to observe from your own engine room, those parts of your business where your best and worst customer service professionals do business every day. You need to see what life is like from where they sit, what they experience every day and what happens when they try to do the right thing for your customers. This is the real *Genchi Genbutsu* opportunity, the chance to go down and see the problem for yourself. This is essential and failure to go inside the business and see what things are really like is one of the leading reasons why so many organisational change programmes fail. Those at the top often don't have a real appreciation of what life is like for employees.

Finally you need to take a helicopter view of the organisation, looking at the organisation from a distance to see what can't be seen at close quarters. Talk to suppliers, and others who don't know you and your business very well to see if they have any interesting and new insights.

Only by acquiring these unique and different insights will you be in a position to drive customer service to where you want it to be.

The seven Ps assessment is designed not only to look at each of the Ps but also to provide all three perspectives required for a complete assessment of customer service delivered by your organisation.

Thoughts on carrying out an assessment

You might only have one shot at improving your reputation for customer service so you need to give yourself the best possible chance. Assumptions are the greatest threats to getting this right. Take the time to plan this properly as a project. Get the right people involved, give it the time it deserves, ask the right questions to the right people, and use what you learn to maximum effect. You can't cut corners to save time or cost because if you do you will signal just how unimportant customer service and customers really are to your business.

Finally, take a leaf out of the book of great change masters and don't be over ambitious. You may learn that you need to change a great number of things. Don't be concerned if this is what you find. Instead decide on the order in which you can realistically do things and start small. Be ambitious but not over-ambitious. Be confident but not over-confident. Be realistic but also cautious. And keep making progress.

A steady, predictable and continuous stream of improvements dotted throughout your customer service system could be the perfect approach to adopt for driving the kind of change you want and delivering the kind of sustained and outstanding service you want to provide to your customers.

Key things to remember

- You can't transform until you know where you are today.
- Get used to looking at the big picture – customer service is a chain and you need to understand the whole chain.
- Generalizing may save time but it will lead you astray.
- Everything begins with your customers.
- Don't just take one perspective, take three.
- Identify your value chain <u>and</u> your customer service system.
- Assess the parts separately and together.
- Look at all seven Ps, not just your people.
- Make sure you know what you are doing and if you are not sure please seek help.

PAUSE AND THINK

How confident are you that you know where you are today when it comes to customer service? When was the last time you asked a customer for honest feedback? Have you looked from different perspectives? Have you been neglecting some of the Ps? Do you know how you will begin?

12 COME UP WITH A PLAN AND SHARE IT

Transformation is a big concept in business today. It is easier to describe and understand than it is to do. In the same way that every business recognizes that change is required for progress, most business leaders find themselves asking how they can engage their employees in the process of change. And that really is the million Dollar question. How does a business leader actually go about changing the customer service system inside their business and making the changes stick?
To keep the process of change as clear and as methodical as possible I will set the process out in step-by-step fashion.

Step 1 – Be clear and precise about what you do and where you are going

Clarity of purpose is where everything begins and ends. If you can't summarize for everyone you meet what the mission of your business is in one or two sentences then you're not ready to make a change. Think about how clear you would need to be if your office building was in immediate danger and you needed everyone to understand how to escape to safety. That level of brevity and precision is what is required when it comes to the mission of your business. Write it down and then read it to people you trust. Ask if they think your mission is clear and precise. If they can't understand why your business exists from what you wrote down then you still have work to do.

When your message is clear you are will be in a position to share it with everyone in your business. You also need to let people know where you are right now as a business. That's the place from where you will all start and improve. When sharing this with your employees also include the immediate and vivid business context. Remember people are intrinsically intelligent and sensible. They can handle the truth and will respect you for your honesty and candor. Trust your instincts and trust your people and in return your people will place their trust in you. You'll also make sure that everyone is starting from the same point.

Step 2 – Establish a common credo

Business performance is not just about who does what by when. It's equally about how things get done. If you are interested in being successful in the long run and really want an enviable reputation then you need to recognize just how important individual behaviour is to your reputation. While you need to create independence and autonomy in your people you also need to be really clear about what is absolutely not allowed. When it comes to ethical and appropriate behaviour you need to clearly draw the line that will not be crossed and make sure everyone knows where that line is. One of the best ways is to come up with your own guiding principles, your credo if you will, and make sure that you hold everyone, yourself included, to the standards you have set.

The guiding principles that set out exactly how your business and your people carry out their work will form the basis for reputation, consistency of performance, and the selection of who stays and who leaves the business. In your leadership team it must become the basis for leadership unity, and help all leaders agree on a common mission and a common way of doing business. If you waver even slightly on the behaviours that you want to see you send a powerful and destructive message that people won't be called to account and you risk destroying your reputation very quickly.

Step 3 - Identify (not select) your future leaders

The people who are prospective leaders will honor the purpose and credo of your business. The important point here is to identify them, to look for those who present themselves through their demonstrated commitment, consistency and behaviour. When looking for future leaders you need to place special focus on commitment. Commitment is why some people are better than others at staying the course. Commitment to the business explains why some are better than others at adhering to the rules and the procedures when it's easier to bend the rules. Commitment is the difference between doing the job right 100% of the time and doing it right most of the time (or when the boss is looking). By looking for those who demonstrate commitment you are making it clear that you are actually asking for their commitment for the times ahead.

A final point on *not* selecting future leaders. Selecting the leaders puts the onus on you as a business owner or senior manager to make the right call on which people can be the leaders of the future. It makes no sense for you to take the entire responsibility for this. Make it clear what people need to do and what they need to demonstrate if they are interested in leadership positions. By all means have a selection process and selection criteria but don't go trawling through the organisation chart looking for high flyers or top performers. If they really are leaders then they will present themselves, assuming that you are paying attention and looking out for them.

Step 4 - Share honestly with your people

Invite your people to participate in the change you are seeking and ask for their commitment. You know already that some will not commit to change and will not want to engage and get involved. In fact, some people might even try to turn others against the change and may rally against your plans. Be ready to manage some people out of the business. Think carefully about the ways in which you can communicate with employees and don't be lazy. It's too easy to send out mass emails or put up posters and flyers. This is not communicating. If you are the business leader and you are serious about change then you need to engage directly with your people by giving them access to you. Let them meet you and question you, give them more detail and let them challenge assumptions that you or they may be holding. Don't pre-judge why they are anxious or reluctant and most of all don't fall for the worn out cliché that people naturally resist change. It's a lazy and judgmental view of the human beings who work hard for you and your customers.

Step 5 – Come out of the ivory tower

Be prepared to ask for real world insight from the customer. Be brave and ask for raw feedback. Invite your customers into your business, the angrier the better. Do everything in your power to find out what is really going on in your employees' world and in your customers' world. Stop waiting for your management team to tell you honestly what the problems are. They won't tell you because they are afraid. Bypass them regularly and ask those working at the customer edge of your business what the big issues of the day are. Ask them what is getting in the way of doing a great job and be ready for really honest feedback. Honour the feedback and the person giving it to you by not taking it personally and by not taking revenge. If you dishonor any piece of feedback you will never get honest feedback ever again. One more thing: Be willing to mix it up a little by announcing some visits to where real customer service is taking place, and by not announcing others. This will allow you to find out if people are doing a great job all the time or just when you show up.

Step 6 - Set out how things really are

Regularly share financial information, business performance data and everything else of importance so that employees are under no illusion about how the business is doing and what they must do now. Don't assume that all data is equally important and for heaven's sake don't bombard your employees with pages and pages of metrics. Do your homework and ask employees what information would be useful to see on a regular basis. Put systems in place to make it easy and quick to get this data. Share the information in simple and easily accessible ways. Come up with a realistic timetable for updates and stick to it. If you are finding that you have bitten off more than you can chew and that you can't get data ready in time let your employees know and reduce the amount of information to be gathered and presented. Make sure that you keep people informed when things are going well and not going so well. And make it clear what they need to do to act on the information. Be very careful not to extrapolate too much from small sets of data. Two points don't make a trend. Be careful not to interpret data too heavily. Reading too much into what the data 'means' could cause you to make costly decisions based on bad guesses. Challenge the data, beware of assumptions and keep it simple.

Step 7 – Simplify the work

Agree on a small core set of simple procedures that govern the way employees should go about their work. Keep it fluid and open to continuous improvement and encourage employees to feed back their suggestions. Do everything in your power to allow employees to make crucial customer decisions up to a reasonable cost limit and become independent problem solvers reducing dependency on management decision-making. Keep an eye on the costs of these decisions and share the info so people can see what is and is not working.

Step 8 - Hold everyone on the team accountable

This includes the entire management team. Use simple systems to make sure all employees can see who is trying and succeeding, who is not succeeding and, most importantly, who is not trying. Decide who will track this, how often it will be updated and stick to it. If you waver with this information any progress you hope to make is assured of death. Devise a language of accountability that everyone can use. Introduce language and expressions that can quickly become part of the way people review progress in meetings. Find a way to call each other to account using direct language that is professional and dignified but which leaves everybody clear on who needs to what and when to remedy non-performance. Remember that accountability is the secret ingredient in making sure customers are served properly and that the business runs profitably. If you let one another off the hook, soon everyone will figure out that performance and standards are nothing but buzzwords.

> As the leader of a business everyone will watch what you do to figure out what they can and can't get away with. If, at your meeting, one of your managers comes to the meeting not having completed an action he promised to complete you can't allow him to brush it off and excuse it away as 'no big deal'. You need to be seen to engage in 'tactful disciplining' by making it clear to him and everyone else that deadlines are to be respected. A firm but fair message from you to him that next week's meeting will begin with his update sends a powerful message that you mean business and that you won't tolerate others not respecting the meeting and its outputs.

Step 9 – Pay attention to successes

Keep a close lookout for any and all successes, especially the little ones at the start. When you come across success stories and examples of employees doing the right thing make sure to let everyone know. Reinforcing the behaviours you want and highlighting the results that matter will be critical for proving to employees that you are serious about doing things right. You don't need to make a big show of recognizing success. In fact a quick call or email or, even better, a quick handshake and a word in the ear to let the person know you noticed their great work is worth more than a big formal recognition event in front of the whole business.

One final point on recognizing people: Try and recognize good work immediately or at least as quickly as you can. Delaying your action means you lose the spontaneity and often employees can't remember doing what you are highlighting. Be spontaneous, be genuine and be timely. It's simple. Remember that your best people care about their work and their customers and ultimately about your business. Be sure to recognize this care and loyalty and repay it using a personalized approach.

Step 10 – Thank your customers too

Don't forget to thank your customers directly every now and then. It can be done using the same formula as before. Be genuine, keep it simple and find an appropriate time to approach a customer. Don't attempt to contact a customer without first checking what you and your organisation have done lately for (or to) that customer. The worst thing in the world is contacting a customer to say thanks only to find out they are currently in dispute with someone in your business. Always do your homework. Prepare what you want to say and stick to it.

Key things to remember

- If you intend to share a plan make sure that it is simple and clear enough to make sense to a 10 year old child.
- Write down how you want things done in credo format and share it with everyone. Display it everywhere.
- Identify the leaders but let them prove they are leaders.
- Be open, honest and candid with your employees. If you don't trust them they can't trust you.
- Visit where the real work gets done on a regular basis and get the unfiltered truth.
- Regularly tell everyone how the business is doing especially when it is struggling.
- Keep processes to a minimum and allow employees to make as many decisions as possible.
- Hold people accountable for their results and recognize all successes, no matter how small.
- Thank everyone, because you really should.

PAUSE AND THINK

When is the last time you asked your employees what they think your plan is? Where do employees learn about how things should be done? What are you doing to show you trust your employees? When have you last held a member of your management team accountable for their results? When did you last thank a customer for their business?

13 MEASURE, CORRECT AND KEEP TRYING

Customer service suffers because of bad habits. We continue to do things that annoy customers and drive them to our competitors. We now know we need to pay attention to these bad habits and start replacing them with good habits. We also know that customers are reasonable and actually want to remain loyal to someone who treats them fairly and consistently. They really don't want to fight and make trouble. They just want us to honor the promises we make. Customers are very well informed and connected so we can't afford to mistreat them or make assumptions about them.

We begin the journey to building great customer service by truly understanding why our business exists and what role customer service must play. This means that as employers, we need to develop a deeper understanding of customers' expectations, and what employees must do to meet those customer expectations. The time for guessing and approximating is over. It's time to go to where the employee meets the customer and learn again.

For a great business with great customer service you must have great people. The focus must be on finding people who really care about their work and making sure these people continue to fit in their roles. Managers have to be on constant watch for great talent, and this talent needs careful handling.

Make sure that your employees understand what is really important. Make sure that they know what causes satisfaction for customers, and what really annoys customers. Ensure that employees know how to use the systems and available resources, and that they know how to behave and react when something goes wrong. Moments of truth, moments where things go wrong and can be corrected, always present an opportunity to create a customer for life.

Create a great organisation and leave your people alone to get on with the work. Reward and recognize exemplary performance and personalize it whenever you can. This means you need to learn as much as you can about your employees. Redefine what promotion means and make it attractive and sustainable for your best employees to keep doing what they love.

You can't change until you know where you are. Invest time and resources to create a full understanding of your customer service system. Take the time to get internal and external perspectives on your business and customer service delivery. This allows you to take the right actions in the right areas to make changes that will make a difference. Be ready to share your plan and be accessible to your employees. This is how they will know that you are serious about change.

Finally, having reached this stage it will important for you to know if your hard work is paying off. To know this you must measure what matters. But what exactly does matter when it comes to improving the customer service experience?

Measure what you want

Quite simply you should measure what is important to you. If you want customers to become more loyal to your business then you need to measure customer loyalty. If you want improved profitability then you need to measure profits. If the number of customer referrals is what you want to increase, then you should measure that. You should measure what you want. Failure to measure what you want will lead to confusion and distress. If you ask employees to do one thing while simultaneously measuring something else your employees will gravitate to doing that which is being measured. Measurement implies that it must be important. Make sure it is.

Hard and soft measures

Try to avoid measuring just hard (financial) or just soft (customer satisfaction) outcomes. Research suggests that you should try and use both hard and soft measures. Clearly you must pay attention to financial outcomes but don't exclusively measure the financials or you will send a message that the softer stuff does not matter. Likewise be careful not to solely measure customer experience without the financials. You could end up signaling that you are willing to forego profit in order to deliver an outstanding customer experience.

Don't be too scientific

Watch out for perfectionist tendencies as you conduct measurements. Aim for a realistic target. You don't want to make an effort at measurement any more burdensome than it should be. If it ends up being too much work to get the simple information you need you will give up. Keep it simple and don't worry about your data meeting academic standards of reliability and validity. Remember you are doing this to learn if your attempts are making any difference to your customers. You don't need massive sample sizes or regression analysis. You just need to know if your efforts are being noticed and whether they are making customers think, feel or act differently towards your business.

Two data points don't make a trend

Be careful not to make huge leaps of interpretation based on very little data. In particular be careful not to assume that a trend exists when you have no more than a few data points. Use whatever information you gather to test assumptions and to inform further questions for your customers and employees. Challenge your own assumptions from time to time, and examine how you are interpreting the data you are gathering.

Although you don't need to be overly scientific, make sure that you bring some rigor to the process of info gathering by using standardized questionnaires, trained staff and a method for analyzing and interpreting data that is consistent over time. There are some wonderful resources out there that make the process of gathering data very simple, especially if you are not experienced in doing so. Visit www.surveymonkey.com or www.polldaddy.com and you'll find some easy to use survey tools that will get you up and running in no time. These are just two examples and a simple Google search for 'create online survey' will yield many other options.

Use every available channel

Be careful not to make stereotypical assumptions about the best way to reach your customers. Resist the temptation to use a single channel such as phone calls or mailed out questionnaires when your customers may be accessible through text messaging or social media tools. Check that you are not choosing channels of communication because you are afraid of what you might hear by using others. Challenge yourself to reach the maximum number of customers using the maximum viable number of channels.

Find the frequency that works

Don't become that annoying business that plagues its customers with irritating surveys and phone calls. Work hard to find the frequency of contact that works for your customers by asking your customers to tell you what they would like. You need to find out when it comes to gathering data from them how often is too often, and how much contact is not enough?

Give it back

When you gather data you need to go back to those you gathered it from and tell them what you learned and what you plan to do as a result. If you don't go back you have disrespected the opportunity that your customers gave you. Would you agree to participate again in data gathering if you never heard back from those who took your information? In particular when you gather data from your customers you need to get back in touch with them to say thanks and to share what you learned. You need to tell them how by helping you now they have made it possible for you to serve them better in the future. They will be more inclined to take part again if they feel they will benefit also. Tell your employees too what you learned and what this means to the business. And finally share the knowledge with your business partners and other stakeholders.

Deal with it without delay

Take action and do it now. It's a major flaw of data gathering exercises to allow data to be gathered, analyzed, and filed and then never see the light of day again. Use the information and use it quickly because, like most things, it has a useful shelf life and then becomes worthless. You will need to protect yourself from misinterpreting your data so consider trials and pilots of ideas that the data suggests to you. Some of the best business ideas can come from misinterpretations of information as long as you don't bet your business on the idea. Try lots of small experiments and see which ones make sense and more importantly make a difference to your customer and your business results. give an example

Keep it simple and keep it going

Don't stop when you think you're there. Many businesses get crucial insight from their customers, take action, and then sit back to admire their work. Competitors will learn too and they will quickly catch up and ultimately pass you out. Just because you have solved a problem doesn't mean everything is complete. Success is fleeting and you need to be on your toes to keep ahead of your rivals. Don't stop because it seems ok. The culture of seems is damaging to your business. When employees start to use the term seems in everyday conversation about customers you should be very worried. If customers seem to be happy about the new opening hours alarm bells should ring in your head. It could be that nobody has actually asked the customers what they think about the opening hours. When managers are telling you that employees seem to be fine with the new incentive scheme you should take that as a big message that nobody has asked the employees.

Seems is a very dangerous word in business. It is another way of describing a lazy culture where details have ceased to be important. Details are always important and you and your staff should strive to have the best customer data in the market. You should strive to know more and understand more about your customers than anyone else.

Keep listening to your customers and keep asking them questions about what they want, need, think, feel and do.

There is no substitute for learning when it comes to business. The business that continues to learn about its customers is the business that earns the right to keep those customers..

Key things to remember

- Measure whatever is important to you but try and measure hard and soft together.
- Don't be too scientific – being too particular will delay you forever.
- Be careful about how you analyze the data – challenge any assumptions you make.
- Use lots of different channels to reach your customers.
- Ask your customers how frequently they wish to be consulted with.
- Share what you learn with customers, staff and business partners.
- Act on what you learn without delay.
- Keep it simple and keep it moving forward – don't stop paying attention to what you can learn from customers.

PAUSE AND THINK

What are you measuring today and how are you measuring it? Are you making things more difficult than they need to be? When did you last share your learning with your customers? How long does it take you to take action? Do people in your business 'seem' to know what is going on when it comes to customers?

CONCLUSION

To deliver a consistently great customer service experience to your customer there are a number of things you and your employees need to actively focus on every day. There are also a few pitfalls to watch out for, things that most businesses are tempted to do every now and then, not realizing that they will really damage the customer service experience. Finally, there are two unavoidable and difficult questions you must answer: (1) Do I really care enough about customer service to put the energy into changing things in my business? ; And (2) When I look at my customer service staff, do I have the right people working for me in those roles?

To help you remember what I think are the 12 key components of consistently great customer service I give you the gift of a picture. The picture illustrates what's involved in delivering great customer service. Why not scan or copy it and pin it on the wall somewhere where you and everyone else can see it all the time.

Let me explain what's going on in the picture.

The person standing on the shore is your customer, eagerly awaiting the arrival of great customer service. To the customer, customer service is a thing, a single over-arching explanation of what they experience when they walk through your doors, visit your website, or speak to your staff. It's what they experience when they experience you and all you do.

You know, however, that customer service is in fact made up of many different things. That's what we've been exploring in these pages. In and around the boat called 'customer service' are all the things that will lead to the customer encountering a great experience. Outside the boat lurks those things that could sink your boat and destroy your attempts to provide your customer with a great experience. Let me jog your memory.

Starting with the dangers outside the boat, the first thing that can prevent the customer experiencing great service is STUPID RULES. Those rules you have that perhaps made sense at one point in time but now just annoy customers and probably staff too. Then you have SELF PRAISE, the tendency that causes businesses to pat themselves on the pack and tell themselves what a great job they are doing, all the time not paying attention to what customers are saying, feeling or doing as a result of your way of serving them. The final rock on which your customer service boat could perish is CHANGE, specifically silly and unnecessary change. All too often we implement change because we mistakenly believe that the only way to improve is to change. Sometimes you already have the winning formula but still you want to change things. These three things happen all the time and they can do huge damage to your best efforts to create a great customer experience.

Let's look at the boat. At the front of the boat sits ANTICIPATION, the capacity to think a few steps ahead of your customer so you can foresee problems and really delight your customer with your thinking ahead. Beside anticipation you have JUDGMENT, specifically good judgment at critical moments. You need judgment to recognize that you are at a moment of truth with a customer, and you need judgment to choose the wise course of action that will keep your customer happy and loyal. Judgment is a leadership trait, and the more you can cultivate this in your employees and the more they develop good judgment the better the customer service experience will be. Next to judgment you find RELIABILITY, the simple act of making promises and keeping them. If you can develop the practice of only setting commitments or making promises that you know you can keep, and then keeping your word you will be well on the way to become unique and trusted in your customers' eyes. You can see RESPECT present here too, because if you don't respect your customers or your colleagues then you'll never be in a position to serve them with excellence. Respect is so fundamental and yet so many people work in customer service roles who have no respect for their customer. Without respect for your customer you'll never achieve the respect of your customer. Everything else falls without respect.

Respecting your customer links strongly to HONESTY, and customers expect that you will be honest in your dealings with them, and in return they will mostly be honest with you. Honesty is a powerful component because it represents a standard or value inside your business. If everyone knows that honesty is critically important and mandatory then nobody will feel the need to try to bend rules or tell lies. There may always be a few rogue employees (and rogue customers) but for the most part good business thrives on honesty.

EMPATHY, the ability to put yourself in the customer's position when it comes to problems, is vitally important. If you can't see things from your customer's perspective then you run the risk of making bad decisions and losing that customer. This takes practice and is a skill worth developing. Empathy has a great defusing power in highly-charged situations and should become a valuable element of your reputation for excellence in service. Linked to empathy, and often as a result of demonstrating empathy we find INSIGHT. By getting to know customers and what they like and dislike you can develop real and meaningful insight. This is hugely important in terms of making what you do more appealing for customers, presenting products, services and information in a way that you know customers will like. It can equally prevent you from wasting time and money on things you know will fail.

Of course, things don't always go according to plan and that's why FLEXIBILITY is a vital component when it comes to great customer service. Linked to good judgment, flexibility is a thing that you have control over, you can choose to bend a little or to make an exception for a loyal customer. Flexibility can be so powerful that a little bit of leeway shown by you for something trivial could result in a loyal customer for life. Making a little effort to help a customer in need when it doesn't cost you much is one of the best marketing tools available to you.

Finally, nothing happens without solid and steady MANAGEMENT making sure people know what they should be doing, getting regular feedback on performance, and driving employees to perform better or exit the organisation.

You may have noticed that I left out one element from the picture. Well that one deserves special mention. The element in question is of course DESIRE. Fittingly it's represented by the engine or motor on the boat, because it is sometimes referred to as 'drive'. Desire is the crucial ingredient that makes the whole thing come together into a great customer service experience. Without desire it's simply not going to happen. You'll recognize this when you encounter someone trying to deliver customer service to you using a script. It feels like you are being processed. While you can train almost all of the other elements so that they come up to the required standard, you can't train someone to have the required desire in order to deliver excellent customer experience. This poses a unique challenge for small businesses everywhere. How can you find those people with the desire to serve customers in the right way, those who want to create memorable customer service experiences every time? The good news is that such people are out there. They may not be working for you, they may not even be working with customers. But they do exist. Your job is to go looking for them, to create the kind of environment that attracts them, to recruit them and retain them, and to support them so that they develop and grow as they go about their task of creating wonderful customer service experiences for your customers.

Even better news may be that you already have these kind of people in your business, but you haven't been paying close attention to them. Such people are prized assets because they have plenty of desire, and as long as you nourish them in the right way their desire will remain strong.

You may notice I have not mentioned money, IT systems, or complex phone systems, or bonuses or anything like that. I did mention training but only to say that you can train some of these elements. In reality you can probably get to the same result by regularly talking to and sharing with your people.

Customer service was never meant to be difficult. Customer service was always meant to be about how people interact with other people, and how much honesty and regard exist in that interaction. We have made it complex over time. We have added all the things that we now know we don't need. We added the complexity so we should be able to remove it too. Let's make customer service simple and real again. And let's channel the desire and talents of great people so that customer service becomes, once again, the reason for choosing your business over your competitor.

REFERENCES

[1] Source: http://www.businessinsider.com/most-hated-companies-america-2011-6?op=1
[2] Mehrabian, A., 1977, *Nonverbal Communication*, Aldine.
[3] Mackay, H., 1988, *Swim with the sharks Without Being Eaten Alive*, Joseph.
[4] Buckingham, M. & Coffman, C., 1999, *First, Break All The Rules*, Simon & Schuster, New York.
[5] See 3 above.
[6] Sieger R., 1999, *Natural Born Winners*, Century, London.
[7] Ekman, P., 1973, *Darwin and Facial Expression: A century of research in review*, Academic Press, London.
[8] Try googling using search terms 'bad customer service forum' and see what comes up.
[9] Porter, M., 1985, *Competitive Advantage: Creating and sustaining superior performance*, Free Press.
[10] Walton, S., 1993, *Sam Walton, Made in America*, Doubleday.
[11] Liker, J., 2003, *The Toyota Way: 14 Management Principles from the World's Greatest Manufacturer*, McGraw Hill Professional.
[12] Maslow, A.H. & Frager, R., 1987, *Motivation and Personality*, Harper & Row, London.
[13] Herzberg, F., Mausner, B., and Bloch Snyderman, B., 1993, *The Motivation to Work*, Transaction Publishers.
[14] Argyris, C., 1991, "*Teaching Smart People how to Learn*", Harvard Business Review 69 No. 3.
[15] Berne, E., 1968, *Games People Play: The Psychology of Human Relationships*, Penguin.
[16] Kaplan, R.S. & Norton, D.P., 1996, *The Balanced Scorecard: Translating Strategy into Action*, Harvard Business Press.
[17] See 11 above.
[18] Senge, P.M., 1990, *The Fifth Discipline: The Art and Practice of The Learning Organization*, Doubleday.
[19] Peter, L.J. & Hull, R., 1969, *The Peter Principle: Why Things Always Go Wrong*, HarperCollins.
[20] Buckingham, M. and Clifton, D., 2001, *Now, Discover Your Strengths*, Free Press.
[21] See 10 above.
[22] Collins, J. C. & Porras, J.I., 1997, *Built To Last: Successful Habits of Visionary Companies*, HarperBusiness.
[23] Reichheld, F., 2003, "The One Number You Need To Grow", *Harvard Business Review* 81, No. 12 (2003): 46-55.
[24] See 9 above.
[25] See 18 above.
[26] Bloom, N. and Van Reenen, J., 2007, "Measuring and Explaining Management Practices Across Firms and Countries." *The Quarterly Journal of Economics* 122, no. 4 (2007): 1351-1408

THE SMALL BUSINESS ADVANTAGE

ABOUT THE AUTHOR

Justin G Kinnear is a native of Dublin, Ireland. An experienced senior leader in various international businesses, Justin has spent his career as a leadership development executive educator, an executive facilitator, a business coach and a professional trainer in various areas of specialism.

www.justinkinnear.com

www.ingramcontent.com/pod-product-compliance
Lightning Source LLC
Chambersburg PA
CBHW051712170526
45167CB00002B/631